THREE POETS OF THE FIRST WORLD WAR

IVOR GURNEY was born in 1890, and was trained in music and singing from an early age. A chorister at Gloucester Cathedral, he was later a student at the Royal College of Music in London. First rejected in 1914 for military service on account of his eyesight, he was drafted into the 5th Gloucester Reserve Battalion in 1915. He saw action on the Western Front, and was discharged from the Army in 1918 suffering the effects of gas and a recurrence of the mental problems that had plagued him before the war. In 1922, after a series of odd jobs and increasingly disturbed behaviour, he was committed to the asylum, first at Barnwood House, Gloucester, then the City of London Mental Hospital in Dartford, where he died in 1937.

ISAAC ROSENBERG was born in 1890 and grew up in Stepney in the East End of London. A painter as well as a poet, he trained at the Slade School of Art, exhibited his work at the Whitechapel Art Gallery, and was friends with a number of influential early twentieth-century artists including Mark Gertler and David Bomberg. Rosenberg, who was in South Africa when war was declared, enlisted in the Army in 1915, and served on the Western Front with the 11th and the 1st Battalions of the King's Own Royal Lancaster Regiment. He was killed on 1 April 1918 near Arras.

WILFRED OWEN was born in 1893 and was brought up in Birkenhead and Shrewsbury. He served as a lay assistant to the vicar of Dunsden before taking up teaching work in France in the year before the outbreak of war. He enlisted in the Artists' Rifles in 1915 and served with the 2nd and 5th Manchesters on the Western Front, where he was concussed and diagnosed with shellshock. Sent to Craiglockhart War Hospital in Edinburgh, he there met Siegfried Sassoon. He returned to the front in September 1918, was awarded the Military Cross, and was killed on the banks of the Oise-Sambre Canal in northern France on 4 November 1918, one week before the Armistice.

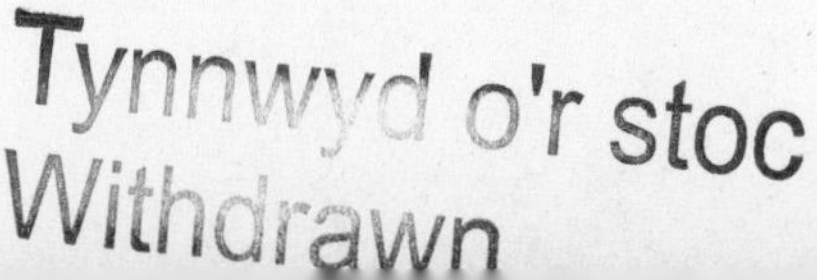

JON STALLWORTHY, FBA, is Emeritus Professor of English Literature at Oxford University and a Fellow of Wolfson College, Oxford. His books include the seven collections of poems selected in *Rounding the Horn: Collected Poems*, and a more recent collection, *Body Language*; two critical studies of Yeats's poetry; two prize-winning biographies, *Wilfred Owen* and *Louis MacNeice*; a fragment of autobiography, *Singing School*; and a collection of essays, *Survivors' Songs: from Maldon to the Somme.* He has also edited Wilfred Owen's *Complete Poems and Fragments*, *The Penguin Book of Love Poetry*, *The Oxford Book of War Poetry* and, with others, *The Norton Anthology of English Literature* and *The Norton Anthology of Poetry.*

JANE POTTER is Senior Lecturer in Publishing at the Oxford International Centre for Publishing Studies, Oxford Brookes University. Her *Boys in Khaki, Girls in Print: Women's Literary Responses to the Great War 1914–1918* was joint winner of the Women's History Network Book Prize. Her recent publications include 'The Bible and the Great War Poets' in *The Blackwell's Companion to the Bible in Literature*, entries for the *Oxford Dictionary of National Biography*, including Jessie Pope and May Wedderburn Cannan, and an edition of the First World War novel *Good Old Anna* by Marie Belloc Lowndes. She is Editor of the *Wilfred Owen Association Journal.*

IVOR GURNEY, ISAAC ROSENBERG *and* WILFRED OWEN

Three Poets of the First World War

Edited with an Introduction and Notes
by JON STALLWORTHY *and* JANE POTTER

PENGUIN BOOKS

PENGUIN CLASSICS

Published by the Penguin Group
Penguin Books Ltd, 80 Strand, London WC2R 0RL, England
Penguin Group (USA) Inc., 375 Hudson Street, New York, New York 10014, USA
Penguin Group (Canada), 90 Eglinton Avenue East, Suite 700, Toronto, Ontario, Canada M4P 2Y3 (a division of Pearson Penguin Canada Inc.)
Penguin Ireland, 25 St Stephen's Green, Dublin 2, Ireland (a division of Penguin Books Ltd)
Penguin Group (Australia), 250 Camberwell Road, Camberwell, Victoria 3124, Australia (a division of Pearson Australia Group Pty Ltd)
Penguin Books India Pvt Ltd, 11 Community Centre, Panchsheel Park, New Delhi – 110 017, India
Penguin Group (NZ), 67 Apollo Drive, Rosedale, Auckland 0632, New Zealand (a division of Pearson New Zealand Ltd)
Penguin Books (South Africa) (Pty) Ltd, 24 Sturdee Avenue, Rosebank, Johannesburg 2196, South Africa

Penguin Books Ltd, Registered Offices: 80 Strand, London WC2R 0RL, England

www.penguin.com

First published 2011
003

Set in 10.25/12.25 pt Postscript Adobe Sabon
Typeset by Jouve (UK), Milton Keynes
Printed in Great Britain by Clays Ltd, St Ives plc

ISBN: 978-0-141-18207-0

www.greenpenguin.co.uk

Contents

Ivor Gurney

Isaac Rosenberg

Wilfred Owen

Dedicated
with affection and gratitude
to the memory of
VIVIEN NOAKES
editor and champion of
Isaac Rosenberg

Chronology

Year	Historical Events	Ivor Gurney
1890		(28 August) IVOR BERTIE GURNEY born at 3 Queen Street, Gloucester, the son of David Gurney, tailor, and his wife Florence Lugg.
1893		
1896		The Gurney family purchases a piano.
1897		
1899		Ivor Gurney joins the choir of All Saints' Church, Gloucester.
1900		Ivor Gurney wins a place in the Gloucester Cathedral Choir and attends King's School; learns the organ.
1904		Gurney sings with Madame Albani at the Three Choirs Festival and begins to write music.
1905		Gurney begins his close association with his godfather, the Rev. Alfred

Wilfred Owen	*Isaac Rosenberg*
	(25 November) ISAAC ROSENBERG born at 4 Victoria Square, Bristol, the son of Barnett (formally Dovber) Rosenberg, pedler, and his wife Hacha Davidar.
(18 March) WILFRED EDWARD SALTER OWEN born at Plas Wilmot, Oswestry, the son of Tom Owen, railway clerk, and his wife Susan Shaw.	
The Owen family moves to Birkenhead.	The Rosenberg family moves to Stepney in London's East End. Isaac is sent to St Paul's School, St George-in-the-East, having been unable to enrol in the Jews' Free School.
	Isaac Rosenberg moves to Baker Street School, Stepney.
(11 June) Wilfred Owen starts school at mid-term at the Birkenhead Institute.	
	(January) Rosenberg apprenticed to Fleet Street engraver Carl Hentschel.

Year	Historical Events	Ivor Gurney
1905 (*contd*)		Cheesman, and Margaret and Emily Hunt.
1906		Gurney becomes an articled pupil of Dr Herbert Brewer, organist of Gloucester Cathedral, and a friend of Herbert Howells, F. W. Harvey and John Haines. Works temporarily as an organist at Whitminster, Hempsted, and at the Mariners' Church in Gloucester Docklands.
1906-7		
1907		
1908		

Wilfred Owen	*Isaac Rosenberg*
	(September) Writes his earliest surviving poem, 'Ode to David's Harp'. His poetic ambitions are encouraged by Morley Dainow, Librarian of the Whitechapel Public Library, who introduces him to the work of Browning, Tennyson, Dante Gabriel Rossetti and Swinburne.
Tom Owen appointed Assistant Superintendent, GW and LNER, Western Region, and the family moves to Shrewsbury.	
	Rosenberg enrols for evening classes at Birkbeck College, London. The Rosenberg family moves to Mile End, East London.
	Rosenberg, Mark Gertler, David Bomberg and Mark Weiner at the Whitechapel Library and Art Gallery, a gathering place for aspiring young East End artists.

Year	*Historical Events*	*Ivor Gurney*
1910		
1911		Gurney wins an open scholarship for composition at the Royal College of Music, is taught composition by Charles Villiers Stanford and makes friends with Marion M. Scott and Ethel Voynich.
1912		
1913		Gurney begins to write poetry seriously. (May) Diagnosed as suffering from dyspepsia and 'neurasthenia' and returns to Gloucester to recuperate. (Winter) Begins his settings of five Elizabethan lyrics, 'The Elizas'.

Wilfred Owen	*Isaac Rosenberg*
The Owen family moves to Mahim, Monkmoor Road, Shrewsbury.	
(9 September) Wilfred Owen takes the University of London matriculation exam. (28 September) Interviewed by the Rev. Herbert Wigan, vicar of Dunsden, near Reading, and is offered an unpaid post as lay assistant and pupil in his Evangelical church. (early October) Hears he has matriculated at the University of London, but not with honours. (20 October) Arrives at Dunsden.	(2 January) Rosenberg meets Joseph Leftowitz and John Rodker and is invited to join their select group of friends known as the Whitechapel Boys. (13 October) Registers as a student at the Slade.
	(Spring/Summer) Rosenberg's first book of poems, *Night and Day*, is privately published. (July) Receives the Slade School of Fine Arts First Class Certificate for the session of 1911–12. His allowances are reduced by his patron, Mrs Cohen, who mistakenly thinks he is not working hard enough. The Rosenberg family moves to Stepney.
(Early January) Owen determines to leave Dunsden and to break with Evangelical religion. (16–19 May) Takes the Reading University scholarship examination, but in July hears he has failed to win it. (*c.* 15 September) Leaves for Bordeaux to teach English at the Berlitz School of Languages.	David Bomberg paints Rosenberg for a portrait entitled *Head of a Poet*, which wins the Henry Tonks Prize. (November) Rosenberg meets the poet T. E. Hulme and arts patron Edward Marsh.

Year	Historical Events	Ivor Gurney
1914	(28 June) Archduke Franz Ferdinand and his wife assassinated at Sarajevo. (28 July) Austria declares war on Serbia. (1 August) Germany declares war on Russia. (3 August) Germany declares war on France and invades Belgium. (4 August) Britain declares war on Germany. (23 August) The British Expeditionary Force retreats from Mons. Germany invades France. (6 September) Battle of the Marne begins. (18 October) First Battle of Ypres.	(4 August) Gurney volunteers for military service but is rejected because of his defective eyesight. (October) Takes a post as organist at Christ Church, High Wycombe, where he makes the acquaintance of the Chapman family. Proposes to Kitty Chapman but is refused.
1915	(19 January) First Zeppelin raid on Britain. (February) British bombard Turkish Forts in the Dardanelles. (23 April) The poet Rupert Brooke dies of sepsis on his way to Gallipoli. (25 April) Allied troops land at Gallipoli. (13 May) The poet Julian Grenfell dies of wounds at Boulogne. (7 May) *Lusitania* sunk by a German U-boat. (23 May) Italy declares war on Germany and Austria. (25 September)	(9 February) Gurney volunteers for the second time, is accepted and drafted into the 5th Gloucester Reserve Battalion, the 2/5th Glosters. Spends the rest of the year in training at Northampton, Chelmsford and Epping. Begins to send Marion Scott his poems.

Wilfred Owen	*Isaac Rosenberg*
(25 July) Owen gives up job at the Berlitz School. (31 July) Travels to Castel Lorenzo, Bagnères-de-Bigorre, High Pyrenees, to act as tutor to Mme Léger, and meets the French poet Laurent Tailhade. (17 September) Returns to Bordeaux with the Légers, and starts to look for pupils as a freelance teacher of English. (4 December) Offered post as a tutor to the two elder de la Touche boys, near Bordeaux.	(May) Marsh buys Rosenberg's painting *Sacred Love*, and Rosenberg exhibits five works in 'Twentieth Century Art: A Review of Modern Movements' at the Whitechapel Art Gallery. (June) Sails for Cape Town, South Africa, to recover his health. Lives at his sister Minnie's house, lectures on contemporary art and takes commissions. Writes 'On Receiving News of the War: Cape Town'.
(October) Owen joins up in the Artists' Rifles, London, moves into lodgings and meets Harold Monro at the Poetry Bookshop. (15 November) Goes to Hare Hall Camp, Gidea Park, Essex, as Cadet Owen, Artists' Rifles.	(February) Rosenberg leaves Cape Town to return to England. (March) Arrives in London. Over the coming months he assembles his second privately published volume, *Youth*, an eighteen-page pamphlet. (October) Rosenberg enlists, reputedly so that his mother would receive his separation allowance. Sent to the Bantam Battalion of the 12th Suffolk Regiment, 40th Division, stationed at Bury St Edmunds. (December) Declines offer of promotion to lance corporal. Two of his paintings and one drawing are accepted for the

Year	*Historical Events*	*Ivor Gurney*
1915 (*contd*)	Battle of Loos begins. (13 October) The poet Charles Hamilton Sorley killed in action by a sniper during the Battle of Loos. (19 December) Start of evacuation of Allied troops from Gallipoli.	
1916	(27 January) Conscription introduced in Britain. (21 February) Battle of Verdun begins. (31 May) Battle of Jutland. (1 July) Battle of the Somme begins. (15 September) First use of tanks en masse at the Somme.	(February) Gurney with 2/5th Glosters to Salisbury Plain. (25 May) Arrives at Le Havre and is sent into the trenches at Riez Bailleul. (8 June) Gurney and 2/5th Glosters move to Laventie. (15 June) Gurney and 2/5th Glosters relieve the 2nd/1st Bucks in the Fauquissart–Laventie sector. Billeted at La Gorgue. (19 July) Gurney and his battalion are placed in reserve for the attack on Aubers Ridge and 'on Rest' at Richebourg, Neuve Chappelle, Robecq and Gonnehem. (27 October) Move south to Albert and the Somme sector.
1917	(1 February) Germany's unrestricted submarine warfare begins. (6 April) United States declares war on Germany. (9 April)	(15 February) Gurney and the 2/5th Glosters moved to the Ablaincourt sector. (18 March) Gurney and his battalion follow the German withdrawal to Caulaincourt

Wilfred Owen	*Isaac Rosenberg*
	New English Art Club winter exhibition.
(27 February–5 March) Owen on a 10-day Army course lodges over the Poetry Bookshop, and shows his poems to Monro. (5 March) Joins Officers' School, Gidea Park. (4 June) Commissioned in the Manchester Regiment. (18 June) Reports to the 5th (Reserve) Battalion, Manchester Regiment, at Milford Camp, near Witley, Surrey. (24 September) Owen and the 5th Manchesters move to Oswestry, under canvas. (29 December) Crosses to France and Base Camp, Étaples, with his regiment.	(January) Rosenberg transferred to the 12th South Lancashire Regiment in Alma Barracks, Blackdown Camp, Farnborough. Continues to work on his play, *Moses*, and the distraction it causes leads him to forget orders for which he receives punishment. (April) Transferred to the 11th Battalion of the King's Own Royal Lancaster Regiment. (May) Receives news of his posting to France and arranges for publication of *Moses: A Play*. (3 June) Arrives in France. At the front line, and around this time writes 'Break of Day in the Trenches'. (December) 'Break of Day in the Trenches' and 'Marching – as seen from the left file' are published in *Poetry Magazine*.
(1–2 January) Owen joins 2nd Manchesters on the Somme near Beaumont Hamel, in a rest area. Assumes command of 3 Platoon, A Coy. (6 January) 2nd	(January) Rosenberg reports sick, and Marsh's efforts to have him transferred to a clerical post come to nothing. (February) Transferred to the 40th Division Works Battalion;

Year	*Historical Events*	*Ivor Gurney*
1917 (*contd*)	The poet Edward Thomas killed in action at Arras. (27 May) French army mutiny. (Late July) The poet Siegfried Sassoon arrives at Craiglockhart. (31 July) Third Battle of Ypres (Passchendaele) begins. The Irish poet Francis Ledwidge killed in action at the Battle of Passchendaele. (24 October) Battle of Caporetto. (20 November) British tank victory at Cambrai. (5 December) Armistice between Germany and Russia signed.	and then on to Vermand. (7 April) Wounded in the right arm and sent to hospital at the 55th Infantry Base Depot, Rouen. (18 May) Back with his battalion, which moves to the Arras front. (23 June) 'On Rest' at Buire-au-Bois; Gurney becomes the platoon's crack shot. (15 July) Gurney transferred to the 184 Machine Gun Company at Vaux. (31 July) In reserve for the Third Battle of Ypres. Battalion moves on to Buysscheure. (10 September) Gurney gassed at St Julien. (23 September) Admitted to the Edinburgh War Hospital, Bangour, where he meets and falls in love with VAD Nurse Annie Drummond, but the relationship does not last. (November) 'Strange Service', 'Afterwards', 'To Certain Comrades' and 'To the Poet before Battle' are published in E. B. Osborn's anthology *The Muse in Arms*. *Severn & Somme* is published by Sidgwick and Jackson. Gurney transferred to Seaton Delaval for a signalling course.

Wilfred Owen	*Isaac Rosenberg*
Manchesters on the move towards the front. (9-16 January) Owen holds dugout in no man's land; his sentry blinded; his platoon exposed in severe frost. (4 February) Arrives at Abbeville for a course on transport duties. (March) Rejoins battalion near Fresnoy; suffers concussion following a fall at Le Quesnoy-en-Santerre, evacuated to Military Hospital at Nesle and moved to 13th Casualty Clearing Station at Gailly. (4 April) Rejoins his battalion at Selency. (12 April) Into the line again at Savy Wood for twelve days. (2 May) Evacuated to 13th Casualty Clearing Station with shell shock. (June) Sent to No. 1 General Hospital, Etretat, and then to Welsh Hospital, Netley, Hampshire. (26 June) Arrives at Craiglockhart War Hospital, Edinburgh. (July) Writes his first contribution to *The Hydra*; becomes its editor. (*c.* 17 August) Introduces himself to Sassoon. (13 October) Introduced to Robert Graves by Sassoon. (28 October) Appears before a Medical Board and is given three weeks' leave pending return to his unit. (9 November) Lunches and dines with Robert Ross at the Reform Club and meets	one of his tasks is to transport barbed wire up into the line. (June) Transferred to the 229 Field Company, Royal Engineers. (16 September) Returns to England for ten days' leave. (10 October) Reports sick and is admitted to the 51st General Hospital. (December) Rejoins his regiment.

Year	Historical Events	Ivor Gurney
1918	(15 July) Second Battle of the Marne begins. (4 October) Germany asks Allies for an armistice. (29 October) German navy mutiny. (3 November) Austria makes peace. (11 November) Armistice signed.	(February) Gurney is granted leave to visit his sick father; is examined for the effects of gas, and moved to Brancepeth Castle, a convalescent depot. (22 April) Returns to Newcastle General Hospital, and is then moved to Seaton Delaval. (8 May) Sent to Lord Derby's War Hospital, Warrington. (19 June) Gurney sends a suicide note to Marion Scott; tells his superiors that he wants to be sent to an asylum because he hears voices. (23 July) Sent to Middlesex War Hospital, St Albans. (4 October) Discharged from the army with a pension of 8*s* 6*d* a week. Returns to Gloucester, works in a munitions factory and worries his family and friends by his erratic behaviour. (11 November) Finishes work in the munitions factory. (7 December) 'The Battalion is Now "On Rest"' is published in the *Spectator*.

Wilfred Owen

Arnold Bennett and H. G. Wells. (24 November) Owen joins the 5th Manchesters at Scarborough for light duties; appointed 'major-domo' of the Officers' Mess, Clarence Gardens Hotel. (4 December) Promoted to lieutenant.

(26 January) Owen's 'Miners' is published in the *Nation*. (12 March) Posted to Northern Command Depot, Ripon. (June) Graded fit for general service; rejoins 5th Manchesters at Scarborough; receives request from Edith and Osbert Sitwell for poems to include in *Wheels 1918*. (15 June) 'Hospital Barge' and 'Futility' published in the *Nation*. (August) On embarkation leave; visits Sassoon, who has been wounded and invalided home, in hospital in London; spends evening with him and Osbert Sitwell; and reports again to Base Camp, Étaples.
(9 September) Arrives at Reception Depot, Amiens, to await the arrival of 2nd Manchesters. (29 September–3 October) 2nd Manchesters launch a successful assault on the Beaurevoir–Fonsomme line. Owen is awarded the Military Cross. (30–31 October) His battalion takes over the line west of the

Isaac Rosenberg

(7 February) Rosenberg is transferred from the 11th to the 1st Battalion of the King's Own Royal Lancaster Regiment. (19 March) battalion moves to the Greenland Hill Sector near Arras. (28 March) Writes to Marsh enclosing his last poem 'Through these pale cold days'. His company moves forward into the front line at Fampoux. (1 April) Rosenberg is killed when the Germans raided the British lines.

Year	*Historical Events*	*Ivor Gurney*
1918 (*contd*)		
1919		(January) Gurney returns to the Royal College of Music, where Ralph Vaughan Williams is his composition teacher. *Severn & Somme* reprinted. (May) Gurney's second volume of poetry, *War's Embers*, is published by Sidgwick and Jackson. (September) Reappointed organist at Christ Church, High Wycombe.
1920		(6 November) Gurney meets Edmund Blunden and Wilfrid Gibson. Though moving in literary circles, he increasingly suffers from nerves and the inability to write.
1922	James Joyce's novel, *Ulysses*, and T. S. Eliot's poem, *The Waste Land*, are published.	(28 September) Gurney certified insane by Dr Soutar and Dr Terry, and admitted to Barnwood House, a private asylum near Gloucester. (October/November) Escapes from Barnwood House but is recaptured after a few hours. (21 December) Transferred to the City of London Mental Hospital at Dartford.

Wilfred Owen | *Isaac Rosenberg*

Oise-Sambre Canal, near Ors, in preparation for an attack across the canal at dawn on 4 November. (4 November) Owen is killed in early morning on the canal bank at Ors. (11 November) News of his death reaches his family in Shrewsbury.

Year	*Historical Events*	*Ivor Gurney*
1926		
1937	David Jones's epic account of life and death on the Western Front, *In Parenthesis*, is published.	(26 December) Gurney dies and (on the 31st) is buried at Twigworth, near Gloucester. The service is taken by his godfather, Canon Cheesman. Howells plays the organ.

Wilfred Owen	*Isaac Rosenberg*
	Reburial of Rosenberg and other soldiers at Bailleul Road East British Cemetery, St-Laurent-Blagny, near Arras.

Introduction

Three young men of the English underclass – Ivor Gurney, Wilfred Owen and Isaac Rosenberg – responded to the news of 4 August 1914 in different countries and in different ways. Gurney, the most patriotic, was, appropriately, in England and on 8 August 'promptly volunteered' but was rejected 'on account of his eyesight'.[1] His response would have had nothing to do with jingoistic feeling for the British Empire, and everything to do with his love for the landscape of Gloucestershire and the music and poetry of his native land. He had been educated as a chorister at King's School, Gloucester, and in 1911 won a scholarship to the Royal College of Music on the strength of his promise as both pianist and composer. Two years later, he set 'Five Elizabethan Songs' to music.

In February 1915, he again visited a recruiting office to volunteer, and this time was accepted. What is probably his first letter as Private I. B. Gurney of B Company, 2/5th Gloucester Regiment, written to his friend and fellow poet, F. W. Harvey, speaks of

> reading the Georgian Poetry Book, and it is this that has made me write to you. Our young poets think very much as we, or rather as we shall when body and mind are tranquil. Masefields feeling of beauty and its meaning strike chords very responsive in ourselves. I found myself remembering old things, old times together as I read 'Biography', and it brought you very near.[2]

One of the young poets whose work Gurney encountered in *Georgian Poetry, 1911–1912*, the first of a series of five annual anthologies with that title, edited by Winston Churchill's secretary, Edward Marsh, was Rupert Brooke. The son of a Rugby School housemaster, Brooke (1887–1915) was a strikingly handsome and charismatic poet, whose physical presence was matched by a sharpness of intellect, charm and wit that affected everyone with whom he came into contact. His poems in this *Georgian Poetry* anthology, 'The Old Vicarage, Grantchester' and 'The Fish', must surely have struck a responsive chord in the patriotic Glosterman who, a month later, wrote to Marion Scott:

> And so Rupert Brooke is dead; still he has left us a legacy of two sonnets which outshine by far any thing yet written on this upheaval. They are as beautiful as music. They are so beautiful that at last one forgets that the words are there and is taken up into ecstasy just as in music.
>
> 'These had seen movement, and heard music; known
> Slumber and waking; loved; gone proudly friended;
> Felt the quick stir of wonder; sat alone;
> Touched flowers and furs and cheeks. All this is ended.'
>
> But the Times Literary Supplement for March 11 quotes two in full; there you must find them.[3]

Writing to Scott in June, Gurney reported:

> Edward Thomas reviewed Brooke's poems in the Chronicle,
> and I got another sonnet out of that –
> Now God be thanked that has matched us with this Hour
> another very good one.[4]

By August, however, his view of Brooke has changed:

> The Sonnet of R.B. you sent me, I do not like. It seems to me that Rupert Brooke would not have improved with age, would not have broadened; his manner has become a mannerism, both in rhythm and diction. I do not like it. This is the kind of work which his older lesser inspiration would have produced. Great

> poets, great creators are not much influenced by immediate events; those must sink in to the very foundations and be absorbed. Rupert Brooke soaked it in quickly and gave it out with as great ease. For all that we have very much to be grateful for; but what of 1920? What of the counterpart to 'The Dynasts' which may still lie within another Hardy's brain a hundred years today?[5]

In the same letter, Gurney includes his sonnet 'To the Poet before Battle', which shows that in 1915 Brooke was incomparably the better poet.

Word of Britain's declaration of war reached the youngest of the three poets, Wilfred Owen, in the French Pyrenees, where he was tutoring an eleven-year-old girl and revelling in a new landscape and a new language. Having failed to get the first-class honours in the Matriculation exam necessary for university entrance, and also failed to make a success of a lay assistantship to the vicar of Dunsden, he was not anxious to return to England, the scene of his failures, let alone volunteer to fight. At the end of August he told his mother:

> I can do no service to anybody by agitating for news or making dole over the slaughter. On the contrary I adopt the perfect English custom of dealing with an offender: a Frenchman duels with him: an Englishman ignores him. I feel my own life all the more precious and more dear in the presence of this deflowering of Europe. While it is true that the guns will effect a little useful weeding, I am furious with chagrin to think that the Minds which were to have excelled the civilization of ten thousand years, are being annihilated – and bodies, the product of aeons of Natural Selection, melted down to pay for political statues. I regret the mortality of the English regulars less than that of the French, Belgian, or even Russian or German armies: because the former are all Tommy Atkins, poor fellows, while the continental armies are inclusive of the finest brains and temperaments of the land.[6]

Owen's initial poetic response to 'the slaughter' was no more creditable than his initial human response. A poem originally called 'The Ballad of Peace & War', later retitled 'The Ballad of Purchase Money', shows a greater ignorance of the issues involved, and less talent, than anything from the pen of the maligned Rupert Brooke:

> O it is meet and it is sweet
> To live in peace with others
> But sweeter still and far more meet
> To die in war for brothers.[7]

This sentiment was to be dramatically reversed, three years later, in the more famous conclusion of 'Dulce et Decorum Est'. 'The Ballad of Peace & War' ends on a Housmanic note:

> Fair days remain for young and old
> And children's cheeks are ruddy,
> Because the good lads' limbs lie cold,
> And their brave cheeks all bloody.

With the start of September, wounded soldiers began to arrive in the Pyrenean town and when, at the end of the month, Owen wrote to his brother Harold, he no longer spoke of 'this deflowering of Europe', still less of 'a little useful weeding'. Under the good influence of a new and valued friend, the poet Laurent Tailhade, he rediscovered the natural compassion he had shown for the poor and the suffering at Dunsden.

> I went with my friend the Doctor Sauvaître to one of the large hospitals one day last week, where he is operating on the wounded. The hospital is in the buildings of the Boys' *Lycée* [. . . . W]e did the round of the wards; and saw some fifty German wretches: all more seriously wounded than the French. The Doctor picked out those needing surgical attention; and these were brought on stretchers to the Operating Room; formerly a Class room; with the familiar ink-stains on floor, walls, and ceiling; now a chamber of horrors with blood where the ink was. Think of it: there were eight men in the room at once, Germans being treated without the slightest distinction from the French: one scarcely knew

> which was which. Considering the lack of appliances – there was only one water-tap in the room – and the crowding – and the fact the doctors were working for nothing – and on Germans too – really good work was done. Only there were no anaesthetics – no time – no money – no staff for that. So after that scene I need not fear to see the creepiest operations. One poor devil had his shin-bone crushed by a gun-carriage-wheel, and the doctor had to twist it about and push it like a piston to get out the pus. [. . .] I deliberately tell you all this to educate you to the actualities of the war.[8]

It would be three years before those 'actualities' found their way into his own poems. In the interval, he bought a copy of the May 1916 reprint of Rupert Brooke's *1914 & Other Poems*, but left no clue as to what he thought of it. He seems likely to have discussed it with his mother, and poignantly expected her to recognize his quotation from Brooke's peacetime poem. 'The Great Lover' in his March 1917 letter from a battlefield Casualty Clearing Station:

> I am in a hospital bed, (for the first time in life.) [. . .] I may be evacuated to Amiens, if my case lasts long enough. For I began to get right again immediately, after getting into those sheets 'that soon smooth away trouble'.[9]

It seems unlikely that Brooke's '1914' sonnets in any way influenced Owen's decision to shoulder a rifle. He did not share the pastoral patriotism that led Brooke, Gurney, Edward Thomas and other 'Georgian' poets to enlist. After his bad experience of England in 1911–12, and his subsequent good experience of France in 1915, he contemplated

> enlisting in the French Army, if they will have me. This I should like much better, I would at least escape the English Sergeants. Everything, even insults (my inefficient fumblings with a rifle will surely bring these down upon me) will be much more bearable in French – after all they will even increase my vocabulary – I shall remain here until I decide what I must do. I have the feeling that

> France will help me to know what I ought to do, and from her soil I shall receive the conviction, that I so much wish for, that to stay out of it all will be wrong.[10]

By mid-July he had decided against the French army but, concerned that a Commission in the British army 'might be a long time in coming',[11] he was thinking he would 'like to join the Italian Cavalry; for reasons both aesthetic and poetical'. Italy, after much bargaining with the Allies and the Germans, had declared war on Austria-Hungary on 23 May. He soon cooled towards the idea of the Italian army, as towards that of the French, and gradually warmed to a vision of himself in the Artists' Rifles: 'Lord Leighton, Millais, Forbes Robertson,' he told his mother, 'were in Artists' Rifles'. He had earlier told her that 'what would hold me together on a battlefield' was 'The sense that I was perpetuating the language in which Keats and the rest of them wrote.'[12] It is clear that Owen's decision to enlist was not prompted by pastoral patriotism so much as by a linguistic patriotism shared with another young poet, who was even further from home when war was declared.

Isaac Rosenberg had been urged by his doctors to seek the sun as a cure for poor health and, specifically, a persistent cough. Consequently, at the beginning of June 1914, he set sail for Cape Town, where his married sister Minnie was living, and there he wrote 'On Receiving News of the War: Cape Town'. He sent this with an undated letter to the editor of *Georgian Poetry*, Edward Marsh, saying:

> By the time you get this things will only have just begun I'm afraid; Europe will have just stepped into its bath of blood. I will be waiting with beautiful drying towels of painted canvas, and precious ointments to smear and heal the soul; and lovely music and poems. But I really hope to have a nice lot of pictures and poems by the time all is settled again; and Europe is repenting of her savageries.[13]

Rosenberg's letter is more humane and perceptive than Owen's to his mother (quoted above). The accompanying poem is similarly more humane and perceptive than Owen's 'Ballad of Peace & War'. It does, however, share with another of Owen's poems drafted that year, '1914', a vision of the regenerative potential of the war much discussed in the early days. Rosenberg's first war poem ends:

> O! ancient crimson curse!
> Corrode, consume.
> Give back this universe
> Its pristine bloom.

Owen's '1914', sketched out in France that year, was completed between October 1917 and January 1918, by which time one might suppose he would have been dissatisfied – to say the least – by the regenerative, seasonal metaphor with which the octet of his sonnet ends: 'But now, for us, wild Winter, and the need / Of sowings for new Spring, and blood for seed.'

Hearing in Cape Town of the *true* harvest of 1914, Rosenberg wrote 'The Dead Heroes', which invites comparison with both Owen and Brooke. Its literary language in general, and Blakean echoes in particular, suggest an Owen-like loyalty to 'the language in which Keats and the rest of them wrote'. At the same time, the poem shows Rosenberg responding to 'the slaughter' with the elevated insensitivity of Brooke – 'Blow out, you bugles, over the rich Dead' ('1914', III 'The Dead'); an insensitivity shared with many other poets, journalists, politicians and preachers in the early months of the war. Another similarity between 'The Dead Heroes' and another of the upper-class patriot's *1914* sonnets, is Rosenberg's three-fold repetition of the word 'England'. Brooke's four-fold repetition of that sacred name, coupled with a celebration of 'English air' and 'an English heaven', make 'The Soldier' virtually a hymn to England.

In the aftermath of Brooke's death, obituaries and the publication of *1914 & Other Poems* in June 1915, his was a voice of which no British poet or would-be poet could have been unaware; a presence to be acknowledged, imitated or rejected, and the differing reactions of his contemporaries are instructive.

Rosenberg would have been made aware of Brooke earlier than most by their powerful patron, Edward Marsh ('Eddie' to Brooke, 'Mr Marsh' to Rosenberg); and the underclass pedlar's son must have been galled by Marsh's preference for the upper-class 'Young Apollo'. No trace of jealousy, however, appears in the sympathetic letters Rosenberg wrote to his bereaved patron following Brooke's death, and no hint of criticism in one written to a South African feminist friend, Elizabeth Molteno, at the same time: 'One of the poets in the "Georgian Poets" has just died at Lemnos. Rupert Brooke who has so wonderful a poem on death in that book will never write more. He was only 27 and was beginning to do great things.'[14] A year later as a soldier on the Western Front, Rosenberg's opinion has understandably changed:

> The Poetry Review you sent is good – the articles are too breathless, and want more packing, I think. The poems by the soldier are vigorous but, I feel a bit commonplace. I did not like Rupert Brooke's begloried sonnets for the same reason. What I mean is second hand phrases 'lambent fires' etc takes from its reality and strength. It should be approached in a colder way, more abstract, with less of the million feelings everybody feels; or all these should be concentrated in one distinguished emotion. Walt Whitman in 'Beat, drums, beat', has said the noblest thing on war.[15]

In other 1916 letters, he speaks of admiring Brooke's 'Town and Country' and 'Clouds' ('magnificent indeed, and as near to sublimity as any modern poem'), but his other poems 'remind me too much of flag days'.[16]

Rosenberg's disillusionment with Brooke's *1914* sonnets is typical of front-line soldier-poets and, indeed, of thousands of soldiers who were not poets. Like Owen, but unlike Gurney, Rosenberg's decision to volunteer was not prompted by pastoral patriotism, and one must ask what prompted him to leave South Africa. His biographer suggests there was no single answer but, rather, a number of factors.[17] He thought Cape Town 'an infernal city' and asked Marsh to 'think of [him], a creature of the most exquisite civilization, planted in this barbarous land'.[18]

South Africa offered Rosenberg the painter – and he had hitherto considered himself primarily a portrait painter – fine subject material, but he failed to get the lucrative commissions he wanted, and began to recognize a commitment to poetry stronger than to painting. Cape Town was no city for a poet, a fact that intensified his nostalgia for London. In February 1915 he came home and in late October enlisted. He told his friend Sydney Schiff: 'I wanted to join the R[oyal] A[rmy] M[edical] C[orps] as the idea of killing upsets me a bit, but I was too small. The only regiment my build allowed was the Bantams.'[19] This reveals the fundamental humanity of the man, to which his poems would later testify; a humanity seldom, if ever, expressed on enlisting by other poets of the period. For some indeed, like the upper-class Julian Grenfell, 'the idea of killing' was positively attractive. 'One loves one's fellow man so much more when one is bent on killing him,' he wrote.[20] What part, if any, Rosenberg's religious beliefs played in his tender-hearted decency is difficult to determine. As a proud but non-practising Jew, his

> early vision of a loving and beneficent God (evidenced in poems such as 'Night and Day') had already hardened by 1912 into the concept of a sterner Being capable of 'shunning' His creatures ('Spiritual Isolation'), or acting with fickleness towards them ('O'er the Celestial Pathways'). His sometimes tyrannical behaviour springs, the poet dares to suggest, from weakness not strength. Later still He is viewed as simply indifferent ('The Blind God'), His blindness towards His creatures' sufferings arousing in the 'tortured' poet a desire to 'cheat' Him ('Invisible Ancient Enemy of Mine').[21]

The author of that passage, Jean Moorcroft Wilson, continues with a revealing analysis of Rosenberg's developing vision of a cruel Female God, rival of the Male, and ends with the persuasive suggestion that this figure, pre-dating Robert Graves's White Goddess by many years, 'was almost certainly an influence on his admirer' and fellow poet.

The God who presides over the expressly war poems Rosenberg wrote in South Africa is Male, but in nothing else conventional.

'On Receiving News of the War' seems to see His authority overthrown, by 'Some spirit old' (presumably female), who

> Hath turned with malign kiss
> Our lives to mould.
>
> Red fangs have torn His face.
> God's blood is shed.
> He mourns from His lone place
> His children dead.

This God is impotent, as powerless as His children to resist the kiss of death. In another poem of this period, 'The Female God', Rosenberg is more explicit: 'You have dethroned the ancient God.'[22] At this stage, however, his idiosyncratic theology is still evolving and, it must be said, confused. In the first stanza of 'The Dead Heroes', the skies that welcome the heroes' spirits are urged to '*Kiss* their exultant eyes'; and, in the last stanza, they are said to have given back their blood 'To win Eternity / And claim God's *kiss*' (my italics). Whereas the kiss in the earlier poem was 'malign', this later one would seem to be benign; and it is unclear whether the Dead Heroes' God is male (as they would have supposed) or female. Rosenberg's bizarre notion of divine osculation had first appeared in his earlier, peacetime, poems, 'In Kensington Gardens' and 'Night and Day':

> I saw the face of God to-day
> And heard the music of his smile [. . .]
>
> I lay upon the sparkling grass,
> And God's own mouth was kissing me [. . .][23]

The Argument introducing 'Night and Day' begins with a clear expression of the poet-prophet's prewar theological quest:

> NIGHT. The Poet wanders thro' the night and questions of the stars but receives no answer. He walks through the crowds of the streets, and asks himself whether he is the scapegoat to bear

> the sins of humanity upon himself, and to waste his life to discover the secret of God, for all.

In late 1914 and early 1915, God's apparent sanctioning of the slaughter in Flanders, or His inability to prevent it, prompted Rosenberg to write three of the most savage anti-God poems in the language: 'God Made Blind', 'The Blind God' and 'God'. Then, having discovered his deity to be 'a rotting God' ('God'), he turned from God to Man and the suffering of 'humanity'.

In the two and a half years that remained to him, he wrote of this with the authority of experience, with a power and a precision absent from his earlier work; and, given the anger of his poems attacking God, with a curious and touching *absence* of anger. In this, they are strikingly unlike some of the poems of Owen, Sassoon and others; and unlike them also in the vitality and good humour of 'Louse Hunting' and 'Break of Day in the Trenches'. Few poets of any war travelled further than Rosenberg from 'The Dead Heroes' to 'Dead Man's Dump' (the titles say it all); from inhumane patriotism and inane theology to the vivid humanity of the poet-painter's voice and eye:

> A man's brains splattered on
> A stretcher-bearer's face;
> His shook shoulders slipped their load,
> But when they bent to look again
> The drowning soul was sunk too deep
> For human tenderness.

Ivor Gurney's religious background and schooling were quintessentially English. His parents were regular churchgoers, and his two godparents clergymen. The younger, more attentive and inspirational godfather introduced him to the work of Hopkins and other religious poets;[24] and when at the age of ten he won a place in the Gloucester Cathedral Choir, the Cathedral Organist and Master of the Choristers gave him a wide knowledge and deep love of religious music.[25]

Despite what might appear to be a traditional religious upbringing, Gurney's view of religion, as of much else, was distinctly untraditional. In September 1915, after seven months in uniform, he wrote to his good friend Marion Scott:

> As to Faith [. . .]
>
> I repose myself on a blind faith that all evil is somehow unavoidable, and therefore necessary, and that in the End a complete explanation of and compensation for the least scrap of evil is to come.
>
> I hate all formal ceremonies and Churches, and my master in all these things is Wordsworth, and my place of worship his. [. . .] The important thing to remember now is that there are no problems now that were not equally urgent two years or 2000 years ago. A Faith which needs reconstruction now will need it often again maybe.
>
> Let us play – the 48.
>
> People who find their Faith shocked by this war, do not need a stronger faith only, but a different one, without blinkers. The whole question is summed up in the last line of the Ab Prelude. 2nd Book. There you will find a complete and compendious summary of all necessary belief.[26]

Gurney enclosed a sonnet with this letter, which is worth quoting, since it is not included in his *Collected Poems* and is more specific than his credo about his Faith:

Satan above the Battle

Think you that he who made the skies was ever
Able before to make a scene accurst
As this one? Nay; now God hath done his worst,
His keenest spite hath poured on Man's endeavour
To live and dream – like Him! Nor would he sever
His countenancing help from Man, nor burst
That bubble of Love; till those, his creatures, had first
Near equalled Him in might. O clever! Clever!
But, Son of God, and Man, what think you of this?
What is your Passion worth? Three days in Hell
Under protection. Poverty, Judas' kiss?

(O Sentiment!) Or can it be you came
Too soon? These daunting triumphs of Science . . . ! Well,
That's all; but were I you I'd burn with shame.[27]

Two better poems, probably written in 1916, reveal a view of God – William Blake's Nobodaddy Father (as distinct from the suffering son) – close to Rosenberg's: 'Some day, I trust, God's purpose of Pain for me / Shall be complete' ('Song and Pain'), and 'The amazed heart cries angrily out on God' ('Pain'). Far from being a God of Love, Gurney's is a God of pain, whose only virtue seems as a source of inspiration: 'Kyrie Eleison, and Gloria, / Credo, Jubilate, Magnificat'.[28]

Gurney was a Man and Poet of Love, even in circumstances arguably more painful than those of any other English-speaking poet of the Great War and its aftermath: his fifteen years in the lunatic asylum. Like Brooke, he was a 'Great Lover' – a celebrant of friends ('To His Love'), of fellow soldiers ('Farewell'), of places ('Above Maisemore'), of dawn and sunset ('Lovely Playthings'), of music ('Schubert') and of literature ('Walt Whitman'). 'Love', 'lovely', 'dear' are among his favourite words, and he shares with Rosenberg a remarkable absence of anger, a humanity and humour, even when remembering 'The Silent One':

Who died on the wires, and hung there, one of two –
Who for his hours of life had chattered through
Infinite lovely chatter of Bucks accent [. . .]

This is a poem for voices, and about voices: the silenced Bucks voice, 'the politest [public-school] voice' and Gurney's own Gloucestershire voice; each offering its individual combination of the poet's greatest loves – language and music. Together, they offer a classic example of the poetry Auden defined as 'memorable speech'.

Wilfred Owen had the most concentratedly Christian upbringing of all notable English-speaking poets of the Great War; more than his public-school chapel-going contemporaries, Brooke, Blunden, Grenfell, Graves or Sassoon. His mother, Susan Owen, the most powerful presence in the family, was a devout and unquestioning Evangelical. When her husband was appointed stationmaster in Birkenhead, the Owens rented a pew in Christ Church,[29] a church strongly committed to the Ministry of the Word. The marked and dated copy of Susan's Bible shows it to have been her principal reading, a habit and a duty soon shared with Wilfred, who in 1902 was enrolled in the Christ Church sunday school.

His childhood and adolescent letters to his mother, when they were apart, regularly give the text of the day's sermon, the hymns that were sung, or end with a pious postscript, as: 'Greet ye one another with a kiss of Charity. Peace be with you all that are in Christ Jesus. Amen. 1 *Peter* V. 14.'[30] It seems likely that Susan hoped her son might find his future in The Ministry, and she played a leading role in what came to be known in the family as 'Wilfred's Church'; as Harold recalled:

> Aided and encouraged by my mother, Wilfred would on Sunday evenings arrange our small sitting-room to represent a church. The table would be moved away, all available chairs collected and arranged for pews, an armchair turned backwards making a pulpit and lectern. At first it was all very simple but as his enthusiasm grew and his imagination took wing, it became more and more elaborate and my mother was kept busy making altar cloths, stoles, and a perfectly fashioned small linen surplice, all most beautifully worked, for she was superb needlewoman. Finally she made a bishop's mitre. This was most extraordinarily effective; it was made from Bristol boards, white and glossy and cunningly enscrolled with gold paint. Wilfred would spend a long time arranging the room, after which he would robe himself and, looking very priestlike in his surplice and mitre, would call us in to form the congregation. He would then conduct a complete evening service with remarkable exactitude and would end by reading a short sermon he had prepared with great care and thought.[31]

It is interesting and surely significant that, while religion played an important part in Owen's early letters to his mother, it played no part at all in his early letters to *himself*, his poems. God is not mentioned before the vicar's 19-year-old lay assistant had arrived at Dunsden in late 1912, and only mentioned then in terms that would have shocked the Vicar:

> Unto what pinnacles of desperate heights
> Do good men climb to seize their good!
> What abnegation to all mortal joys,
> What vast abstraction from the world is theirs!
> O what insane abuses, desperate pangs,
> Annihilations of the Self, soul-suicides,
> They wreak upon themselves to purchase – GOD!
> A God to guide through these poor temporal days
> Their comings, goings, workings of the heart,
> Obsess, indeed, their natures utterly;
> Meanwhile preparing, as in recompense,
> Mansions celestial for their timeless bliss.
> And to what end this Holiness; this God
> That arrogates their intellect and soul?
> To none! Their offered lives are not so grand,
> So active, or so sweet as many a one's
> That is undedicated, being reason-swayed;
> And their sole mission is to drag, entice
> And push mankind to those same cloudy crags
> Where they first breathed the madness-giving air
> That made them feel as angels, that are less than men.[32]

God rates no more than a rare mention in Owen's poems of 1912–17,[33] and thereafter appears in a guise that the vicar of Dunsden would have found even more shocking: 'But when we're duly white-washed, being dead, / The race will bear Field Marshall God's inspection.'

The anger audible in the caricature of Owen's 'Inspection' no doubt owes much to the influence of his new friend, Siegfried Sassoon, whose poems 'Stand-to: Good Friday Morning' and 'They' he had just read, and whose unpublished 'Christ and the Soldier' he might have been shown.[34] Even had he not seen that, he could have been in no doubt about Sassoon's savagely anti-Christian, anti-clerical views at this time. They were, anyway, a continuation of his own, as expressed to his mother before he had met Sassoon:

> Send an English Testament to his Grace of Canterbury, and let it consist of that one sentence, at which he winks his eyes:
>
> 'Ye have heard that it *hath* been said: An eye for an eye, and a tooth for a tooth:
>
> But I say that ye resist not evil, but whosoever shall smite thee on thy right cheek, turn to him the other also.'
>
> And if his reply be 'Most unsuitable for the present distressing moment, my dear lady! But I trust that in God's good time . . . etc.' – *then there is only one possible conclusion*, that there are no more Christians at the present moment than there were at the end of the first century.
>
> While I wear my star and eat my rations, I continue to take care of my Other Cheek; and, thinking of the eyes I have seen made sightless, and the bleeding lad's cheeks I have wiped, I say: Vengeance is mine, I, Owen, will repay.
>
> Let my lords turn to the people when they say 'I believe in . . . Jesus Christ', and we shall see as dishonest a face as ever turned to the East, bowing, over the Block at Tyburn.[35]

There was, and would remain, one crucial difference between Owen and Sassoon at this time. While they were united in their condemnation of the national established church, Owen would never lose his belief – as Sassoon seemed to for a while – in the person and teachings of Christ.[36] Earlier in 1917, Owen had written to his mother from France: 'Christ is literally in no man's land. There men often hear His voice: Greater love hath no man than this, that a man lay down his life – for a friend.'[37] Christ had made a first – dramatic but ambiguous – appearance in Owen's poetry two years before, as he remembered an Easter 1914 service in Mérignac:

> Then I, too, knelt before that acolyte.
> Above the crucifix I bent my head:

> The Christ was thin, and cold, and very dead:
> And yet I bowed, yea, kissed – my lips did cling.
> (I kissed the warm live hand that held the thing.)[38]

Jesus Christ is frequently named in Owen's poems of 1917–18,[39] and usually more positively than God. The Father is, at best, presented neutrally: 'God will grow no talons at his heels' ('Arms and the Boy'); but more often, as uncaring: 'God seems not to care', and 'love of God seems dying' ('Greater Love' and 'Exposure'). Most tellingly, Father and Son are shown at odds in 'Soldier's Dream', where an act of compassion by 'kind Jesus' is nullified by a 'vexed' God, who instructs his warrior archangel to continue the soldiers' suffering.

Having witnessed and, indeed, shared that suffering, Owen ('a conscientious objector with a very seared conscience')[40] nevertheless implicitly presents himself in the role of the warrior archangel:

> For 14 hours yesterday I was at work – teaching Christ to lift his cross by numbers, and how to adjust his crown; and not to imagine he thirst till after the last halt; I attended his Supper to see that there were no complaints; and inspected his feet to see that they should be worthy of the nails. I see to it that he is dumb and stands to attention before his accusers. With a piece of silver I buy him every day, and with maps I make him familiar with the topography of Golgotha.[41]

Owen's prose has here the controlled passion, richness of metaphor and musical cadencing of his poems, and it shows what distinguishes them from the poems of Gurney and Rosenberg. All three turn away from a distant God able to permit – perhaps again to *cause* – the suffering of His Son/sons. Turning from God, these poets celebrate fallen Man's humanity, as well as chronicling his inhumanity, in the most inhuman of conceivable circumstances. Owen alone, however, continues to believe in the coexistence of divinity and humanity in the person of his great exemplar, Jesus Christ. Associated with that belief, his belief in the responsibility of the true Poet to be truthful, in the role of witness that imposed on him, gave his poems the authority and power to resonate across the years in 'fresher fields than Flanders' ('Preface').

NOTES

For full bibliographical details, see Further Reading.

1. Scott, 'Ivor Gurney: The Man', 4.
2. R. K. R. Thornton, ed., *Ivor Gurney: War Letters* (London, 1984), p. 25. It is easy to see why the vivid seagoing passages in Masefield's long poem should have appealed to Gurney, who enjoyed few things more than sailing his boat *Dorothy* on the River Severn. The 'Georgian Poetry Book' is E[dward] M[arsh], ed., *Georgian Poetry, 1911–1912* (London, 1912).
3. Ibid., p. 29. The quotation is from Brooke's '1914', IV 'The Dead'.
4. Ibid., p. 31.
5. Ibid., p. 34.
6. Owen and Bell, p. 282. For 'annihilated', Owen first wrote 'snuffed out'.
7. Stallworthy, pp. 503–7.
8. Owen and Bell, pp. 284–5.
9. Ibid., p. 443.
10. Harold Owen's recollection of a letter that has not survived, from H. Owen, III, 120–21.
11. Owen and Bell, p. 347.
12. Ibid., 347, 300.
13. Noakes, *Rosenberg*, p. 262.
14. Ibid., p. 273. Noakes notes that the 'poem on death' is 'The Soldier', which cannot be correct, as that appeared in *Georgian Poetry, 1913–1915*, published in November 1915. The poem Rosenberg had in mind is probably 'Dust'.
15. Ibid., p. 304.
16. Ibid., pp. 309, 319, 309.
17. Moorcroft Wilson, pp. 240–46.
18. Noakes, *Rosenberg*, pp. 259–60.
19. Ibid., p. 280.

20. Nicholas Mosley, *Julian Grenfell: His Life and the Times of His Death: 1888–1915* (London, 1976), p. 241.
21. Moorcroft Wilson, p. 234.
22. Noakes, *Rosenberg*, pp. 72–3.
23. Ibid., pp. 25 and 45. Their dates of composition are unknown.
24. The Rev. Alfred Cheesman. See Blevins, pp. 54–6, 86.
25. Dr Herbert Brewer. See ibid., 19–20, 57, 60–62.
26. Thornton, *Ivor Gurney: War Letters*, p. 36. 'The 48' are J.S. Bach's Forty-eight Preludes and Fugues – *Das Wohltemperierte Clavier* (*The Well-Tempered Clavier*), which consists of two books/sets of preludes and fugues; it is the A flat prelude (no. 17) of the second set to which Gurney is referring.
27. Ibid., p. 37.
28. 'There Was Such Beauty', Kavanagh, p. 64.
29. Hibberd, *Wilfred Owen: A New Biography*, p. 18.
30. Owen and Bell, p. 36.
31. H. Owen, I, 150–51.
32. Stallworthy, *Poems*, p. 40.
33. Ibid., pp. 46, 47, 52, 53 and 68.
34. Rupert Hart-Davies, ed., *Siegfried Sassoon: The War Poems* (London, 1983), pp. 28 and 57; 45–6.
35. Owen and Bell, pp. 483–4.
36. See 'Christ and the Soldier', in Stallworthy, *Survivors' Songs*, pp. 55–67.
37. Owen and Bell, p. 461.
38. 'Maundy Thursday', Stallworthy, *Poems*, p. 86.
39. Ibid., pp. 42, 99, 103, 111, 145 and 159.
40. Owen and Bell, p. 461.
41. Ibid., p. 562.

Further Reading

Abbreviations in parentheses are used in notes.

IVOR GURNEY

Editions

Ivor Gurney: 'Best Poems' and 'The Book of Five Makings', ed. R. K. R. Thornton and George Walter (Manchester, 1999)
Ivor Gurney: Collected Poems, ed. P. J. Kavanagh (Manchester, 1984) (Kavanagh)
Ivor Gurney: Collected Letters, ed. R. K. R. Thornton (Manchester, 1991) (Thornton)

Bibliography

Ivor Gurney: Towards a Bibliography, ed. R. K. R. Thornton and George Walter (Hay-on-Wye, 1996)

Biography

Blevins, Pamela, *Ivor Gurney and Marion Scott: Song of Pain and Beauty* (Rochester, NY and Woodbridge, Suffolk, 2008)
Hurd, Michael, *The Ordeal of Ivor Gurney* (Oxford, 1978)
Scott, Marion, 'Ivor Gurney: The Man', *Music and Letters*, 19:1 (January 1938), 2–7

Criticism

Grey, Piers, *Marginal Men: Edward Thomas, Ivor Gurney, J. R. Ackerley* (Basingstoke, 1991)
Hawlin, Stephen, 'Ivor Gurney's Creative Reading of Walt Whitman: Thinking of Paumanok', *English Literature in Transition*, 49:1 (2006), 31–48
Hill, Geoffrey, '"Gurney's Hobby"', *Essay in Criticism: A Quarterly Journal of Literary Criticism*, 34:2 (1984), 97–128
Kendall, Tim, 'Gurney and Fritz', *Essays in Criticism: A Quarterly Journal of Literary Criticism*, 59:2 (2009), 142–56
Rawling, Eleanor M., *Ivor Gurney's Gloucestershire: Exploring Poetry and Place* (Stroud, 2011)
Underhill, Hugh, 'Ivor Gurney', *English Association Bookmarks*, No. 51 (Leicester, 2007)

ISAAC ROSENBERG

Editions

Isaac Rosenberg, ed. Vivien Noakes (Oxford, 2008) (Noakes, *Rosenberg*)
The Poems and Plays of Isaac Rosenberg, ed. Vivien Noakes (Oxford, 2004) (Noakes)
The Collected Works of Isaac Rosenberg: Poetry, Prose, Letters, Paintings, and Drawings, ed. Ian Parsons, with a foreword by Siegfried Sassoon (London, 1979, 1984)

Biography

Cohen, Joseph, *Journey to the Trenches: The Life of Isaac Rosenberg, 1890–1918* (London, 1975)
Liddiard, Jean, *Isaac Rosenberg: The Half Used Life* (London, 1975)
Maccoby, Deborah, *God Made Blind: Isaac Rosenberg, His Life and Poetry* (Northwood, Middlesex, 1999)
Moorcroft Wilson, Jean, *Isaac Rosenberg: The Making of a Great War Poet. A New Life* (London, 2008)

Criticism

Al-Joulan, Nayef, *Essenced to Language: The Margins of Isaac Rosenberg* (New York, 2007)

WILFRED OWEN

Editions

Wilfred Owen: The Complete Poems and Fragments, ed. Jon Stallworthy, 2 vols. (Oxford, 1983) (Stallworthy)

The Poems of Wilfred Owen, ed. Jon Stallworthy (London, 1985) (Stallworthy, *Poems*)

Wilfred Owen: War Poems and Others, ed. Dominic Hibberd (London, 1973) (Hibberd)

The Collected Poems of Wilfred Owen, ed. with an Introduction and Notes by c. Day Lewis (London, 1963)

The Poems of Wilfred Owen, ed. with a Memoir by Edmund Blunden (London, 1931) (Blunden)

Owen, Wilfred, *Poems*, with an Introduction by Siegfried Sassoon (London, 1920)

Wilfred Owen: Selected Letters, ed. John Bell (Oxford, 1985)

Wilfred Owen: Collected Letters, ed. Harold Owen and John Bell (Oxford, 1967) (Owen and Bell)

Biography

Hibberd, Dominic, *Wilfred Owen: A New Biography* (London, 2002)

Owen, Harold, *Journey from Obscurity: Memoirs of the Owen Family*, 3 vols. (Oxford, 1963–65) (H. Owen)

Stallworthy, Jon, *Wilfred Owen* (Oxford, 1974) (Stallworthy, *Owen*)

Criticism

Bäckman, Sven, *Tradition Transformed: Studies in the Poetry of Wilfred Owen* (Lund, 1979)

Hibberd, Dominic, *Owen the Poet* (Basingstoke, 1986)
Kerr, Douglas, *Wilfred Owen's Voices: Language and Community* (Oxford, 1993)
Welland, Dennis, *Wilfred Owen: A Critical Study*, rev. edn. (London, 1978)
Williams, Merryn, *Wilfred Owen* (Bridgend, 1993)

General Reading

Bergonzi, Bernard, *Heroes' Twilight: A Study of the Literature of the Great War*, 3rd edn. (Manchester, 1996)
Booth, Allyson, *Postcards from the Trenches: Negotiating the Space between Modernism and the First World War* (Oxford, 1996)
Caesar, Adrian, *Taking It Like a Man: Suffering, Sexuality, and the War Poets: Brooke, Sassoon, Owen, Graves* (Manchester, 1993)
Das, Santanu, *Touch and Intimacy in First World War Literature* (Cambridge, 2006)
Fussell, Paul, *The Great War and Modern Memory* (London and Oxford, 1975)
Graham, Desmond, *The Truth of War: Owen, Blunden and Rosenberg* (Manchester, 1984)
Hibberd, Dominic, and John Onions, eds., *The Winter of the World: The Poems of the First World War* (London, 2007)
Hipp, Daniel, *The Poetry of Shellshock: Wartime Trauma and Healing in Wilfred Owen, Ivor Gurney and Siegfried Sassoon* (Jefferson, NC and London, 2005)
Hynes, Samuel, *A War Imagined: The First World War and English Culture* (New York, 1990)
Kendall, Tim, *Modern English War Poetry* (Oxford, 2006)
Kendall, Tim, ed., *The Oxford Handbook of British and Irish War Poetry* (Oxford, 2007)
Longley, Edna, 'War Pastorals', in *The Oxford Handbook of British and Irish War Poetry*, ed. Tim Kendall (Oxford, 2009)
Noakes, Vivien, ed., *Voices of Silence: The Alternative Book of First World War Poetry* (Stroud, 2006)

Potter, Jane, 'The Great War Poets', in *The Blackwell Companion to the Bible in Literature*, ed. R. Lemon et al. (Oxford, 2009)

Puissant, Susanne Christine, *Irony and the Poetry of the First World War* (Houndsmill, Basingstoke, 2009)

Quinn, Patrick J., *Recharting the Thirties* (Selinsgrove and London, 1996)

Ramazani, Jahan, *Poetry of Mourning: The Modern Elegy from Hardy to Heaney* (Chicago, 1994)

Sherry, Vincent, ed., *The Cambridge Companion to the Literature of the First World War* (Cambridge, 2005)

Silkin, Jon, *Out of Battle: The Poetry of the Great War* (London, 1972)

Stallworthy, Jon, *Anthem for Doomed Youth: Twelve Soldier Poets of the First World War* (London, 2002)

Stallworthy, Jon, *Survivors' Songs: From Maldon to the Somme* (Cambridge, 2008)

Strachan, Hew, *The Oxford Illustrated History of the First World War* (Oxford, 2000)

Todman, Dan, *The Great War: Myth and Memory* (London, 2005)

Winter, Jay, *Sites of Memory, Sites of Mourning: The Great War in European Cultural History* (Cambridge, 1995)

Editorial Note

Invited to make a selection of poems by Gurney, Rosenberg and Owen, we have chosen those that we hope show their work to the best advantage. The poems are arranged in chronological order, to the best of our inevitably incomplete knowledge.

In the case of the two poets killed in the Great War, our copy-texts are Noakes's 2004 edition of *The Poems and Plays of Isaac Rosenberg* and Stallworthy's 1983 edition of *Wilfred Owen: The Complete Poems and Fragments* (see Notes on the Texts for those poets and Further Reading). There exists at present no comparable complete edition of Gurney's more extensive (and complicated) body of work, though one is now being prepared by Professor Tim Kendall and Philip Lancaster. We have been fortunate to have their advice in the dating and ordering of Gurney's manuscripts, typescripts (frequently from hands other than his) and autograph revisions to printed texts. This research has resulted in some emendation of our copy-texts, Gurney's two published volumes *Severn and Somme* (1917) and *War's Embers* (1919), and P. J. Kavanagh's 1984 edition *Ivor Gurney: Collected Poems* (see Note on the Texts for Gurney and Further Reading).

We have retained the occasional eccentricity – even irregularity – in the capitalization, punctuation, and spelling of poems and prose (quoted in Notes) by all three authors. *Authorial* ellipses we distinguish from *editorial* ones, framing the latter with square brackets to indicate an editorial omission of a word or words; an exception to this rule will be found in the italicized cue-words, where an editorial omission is so self-evident as to need no square-bracketing. Biblical quotations are all taken from the King James Version.

IVOR GURNEY

To the Poet before Battle

Now, Youth, the hour of thy dread passion comes;
Thy lovely things must all be laid away;
And thou, as others, must face the riven day
Unstirred by the tattle and rattle of rolling drums,
Or bugles' strident cry. When mere noise numbs
The sense of being, the fear-sick soul doth sway,
Remember thy great craft's honour, that they may say
Nothing in shame of Poets. Then the crumbs
Of praise the little versemen joyed to take
Shall be forgotten; then they must know we are,
For all our skill in words, equal in might
And strong of mettle as those we honoured; make
The name of Poet terrible in just War,
And like a crown of honour upon the fight.

Strange Service

Little did I dream, England, that you bore me
Under the Cotswold Hills beside the water meadows,
To do you dreadful service, here, beyond your borders
And your enfolding seas.

I was a dreamer ever, and bound to your dear service,
Meditating deep, I thought on your secret beauty,
As through a child's face one may see the clear spirit
Miraculously shining.

Your hills not only hills, but friends of mine and kindly,
Your tiny knolls and orchards hidden beside the river
Muddy and strongly-flowing, with shy and tiny streamlets
Safe in its bosom.

Now these are memories only, and your skies and rushy
sky-pools
Fragile mirrors easily broken by moving airs. . . .
In my deep heart for ever goes on your daily being,
And uses consecrate.

Think on me too, O Mother, who wrest my soul to
serve you
In strange and fearful ways beyond your encircling waters;
None but you can know my heart, its tears and sacrifice,
None, but you, repay.

Bach and the Sentry

Watching the dark my spirit rose in flood
On that most dearest Prelude of my delight.
The low-lying mist lifted its hood,
The October stars showed nobly in clear night.

When I return, and to real music-making,
And play that Prelude, how will it happen then?
Shall I feel as I felt, a sentry hardly waking,
With a dull sense of No Man's Land again?

Song and Pain

Out of my Sorrow have I made these songs,
Out of my sorrow;
Though somewhat of the making's eager pain
From Joy did borrow.

Some day, I trust, God's purpose of Pain for me
Shall be complete,
And then – to enter in the House of Joy. . . .
Prepare, my feet.

Song

Only the wanderer
Knows England's graces,
Or can anew see clear
Familiar faces.

And who loves Joy as he
That dwells in shadows?
Do not forget me quite,
O Severn meadows.

Ballad of the Three Spectres

As I went up by Ovillers
In mud and water cold to the knee,
There went three jeering, fleering spectres,
That walked abreast and talked of me.

The first said, 'Here's a right brave soldier
That walks the dark unfearingly;
Soon he'll come back on a fine stretcher,
And laughing for a Nice Blighty.'

The second, 'Read his face, old comrade,
No kind of lucky chance I see;
One day he'll freeze in mud to the marrow,
Then look his last on Picardie.'

Though bitter the word of these first twain
Curses the third spat venomously;
'He'll stay untouched till the war's last dawning,
'Then live one hour of agony.'

Liars the first two were. Behold me
At sloping arms by one – two – three:
Waiting the time I shall discover
Whether the third spake verity.

Time and the Soldier

How slow you move, old Time;
Walk a bit faster!
Old fool, I'm not your slave. . . .
Beauty's my master!

You hold me for a space. . . .
What are you, Time?
A ghost, a thing of thought,
An easy rhyme.

Some day I shall again,
For all your scheming,
See Severn valley clouds
Like banners streaming.

And walk in Cranham lanes,
By Maisemore go. . . .
But, fool, decrepit Fool,
You are SO SLOW!!!

After-Glow

(To F. W. Harvey)

Out of the smoke and dust of the little room
With tea-talk loud and laughter of happy boys,
I passed into the dusk. Suddenly the noise
Ceased with a shock, left me alone in the gloom,
To wonder at the miracle hanging high

Tangled in twigs, the silver crescent clear. –
Time passed from mind. Time died; and then we were
Once more at home together, you and I.

The elms with arms of love wrapped us in shade
Who watched the ecstatic West with one desire,
One soul uprapt; and still another fire
Consumed us, and our joy yet greater made:
That Bach should sing for us, mix us in one
The joy of firelight and the sunken sun.

Requiem

Pour out your light, O stars, and do not hold
    Your loveliest shining from earth's outworn shell –
Pure and cold your radiance pure and cold
    My dead friend's face as well.

Pain

Pain, pain continual; pain unending;
Hard even to the roughest, but to those
Hungry for beauty. . . . Not the wisest knows,
Nor most pitiful-hearted, what the wending
Of one hour's way meant. Grey monotony lending
Weight to the grey skies, grey mud where goes
An army of grey bedrenched scarecrows in rows
Careless at last of cruellest Fate-sending.
Seeing the pitiful eyes of men foredone,
Or horses shot, too tired merely to stir,
Dying in shell-holes both, slain by the mud.
Men broken, shrieking even to hear a gun. –
Till pain grinds down, or lethargy numbs her,
The amazed heart cries angrily out on God.

Servitude

If it were not for England, who would bear
This heavy servitude one moment more?
To keep a brothel, sweep and wash the floor
Of filthiest hovels were noble to compare
With this brass-cleaning life. Now here, now there
Harried in foolishness, scanned curiously o'er
By fools made brazen by conceit, and store
Of antique witticisms thin and bare.

Only the love of comrades sweetens all,
Whose laughing spirit will not be outdone.
As night-watching men wait for the sun
To hearten them, so wait I on such boys
As neither brass nor Hell-fire may appal,
Nor guns, nor sergeant-major's bluster and noise.

Turmut-Hoeing

I straightened my back from turmut-hoeing
  And saw, with suddenly opened eyes,
Tall trees, a meadow ripe for mowing,
  And azure June's cloud-circled skies.

Below, the earth was beautiful
  Of touch and colour, fair each weed,
But Heaven's high beauty held me still,
  Only of music had I need.

And the white-clad girl at the old farm,
  Who smiled and looked across at me,
Dumb was held by that strong charm
  Of cloud-ships sailing a foamless sea.

Ypres – Minsterworth
(To F. W.H.)

Thick lie in Gloucester orchards now
    Apples the Severn wind
With rough play tore from the tossing
    Branches, and left behind
Leaves strewn on pastures, blown in hedges,
    And by the roadway lined.

And I lie leagues on leagues afar
    To think how that wind made
Great shoutings in the wide chimney,
    A noise of cannonade –
Of how the proud elms by the signpost
    The tempest's will obeyed –

To think how in some German prison
    A boy lies with whom
I might have taken joy full-hearted
    Hearing the great boom
Of Autumn, watching the fire, talking
    Of books in the half gloom.

O wind of Ypres and of Severn
    Riot there also, and tell
Of comrades safe returned, home-keeping
    Music and Autumn smell.
Comfort blow him and friendly greeting,
    Hearten him, wish him well!

To His Love

He's gone, and all our plans
 Are useless indeed.
We'll walk no more on Cotswold
 Where the sheep feed
 Quietly and take no heed.

His body that was so quick
 Is not as you
Knew it, on Severn river
 Under the blue
 Driving our small boat through.

You would not know him now . . .
 But still he died
Nobly, so cover him over
 With violets of pride
 Purple from Severn side.

Cover him, cover him soon!
 And with thick-set
Masses of memoried flowers –
 Hide that red wet
 Thing I must somehow forget.

Photographs
(To Two Scots Lads)

Lying in dug-outs, joking, wearily;
 Watching the candle guttering in the draught;
Hearing the great shells go high over us, eerily
 Singing; how often have I turned over, and laughed

With pity and pride, photographs of all colours,
    All sizes, subjects: khaki brothers in France;
Or mothers' faces worn with countless dolours;
    Or girls whose eyes were challenging and must dance,

Though in a picture only, common cheap
    Ill-taken card; and children – frozen, some
(Babies) waiting on Dicky-bird to peep
    Out of the handkerchief that is his home

(But he's so shy!). And some with bright looks, calling
    Delight across the miles of land and sea,
That not the dread of barrage suddenly falling
    Could quite blot out – not mud nor lethargy.

Smiles and triumphant careless laughter. O
    The pain of them, wide Earth's most sacred things!
Lying in dugouts, hearing the great shells slow
    Sailings mile-high, the heart mounts higher and sings.

But once – O why did he keep that bitter token
    Of a dead Love? – that boy, who suddenly moved,
Showed me, his eyes wet, his low talk broken,
    A girl who better had not been beloved.

To the Prussians of England

When I remember plain heroic strength
Arid shining virtue shown by Ypres pools,
Then read the blither written by knaves for fools
In praise of English soldiers lying at length,
Who purely dream what England shall be made
Gloriously new, free of the old stains
By us, who pay the price that must be paid,
Will freeze all winter over Ypres plains.
Our silly dreams of peace you put aside

And Brotherhood of man, for you will see
An armed Mistress, braggart of the tide,
Her children slaves, under your mastery.
We'll have a word there too, and forge a knife,
Will cut the cancer threatens England's life.

Crickley Hill

The orchis, trefoil, harebells nod all day,
High above Gloucester and the Severn Plain.
Few come there, where the curlew ever and again
Cries faintly, and no traveller makes stay,
Since steep the road is,
And the villages
Hidden by hedges wonderful in late May.

At Buire-au-Bois a soldier wandering
The lanes at evening talked with me and told
Of gardens summer blessed, of early spring
In tiny orchards, the uncounted gold
Strewn in green meadows,
Clear cut shadows
Black on the dust and gray stone mellow and old.

But these were things I knew, and carelessly
Heard, while in thought I went with friends on roads
White in the sun, or wandered far to see
The scented hay come homeward in warm loads.
Hardly I heeded him;
While the coloured dim
Evening brought stars and lights in small abodes.

When on a sudden, 'Crickley' he said. How I started
At that old darling name of home! and turned
Fell into a torrent of words warm-hearted

Till clear above the stars of summer burned
In velvety smooth skies.
We shared memories,
And the old raptures from each other learned.

O sudden steep! O hill towering above!
Chasm from the road falling suddenly away!
Sure no two men talked of you with more love
Than we that tender-coloured ending of day.
(O tears! Keen pride in you!)
Feeling the soft dew,
Walking in thought another Roman way.

You hills of home, woodlands, white roads and inns
That star and line our darling land, still keep
Memory of us; for when first day begins
We think of you and dream in the first sleep
Of you and yours –
Trees, bare rock, flowers
Daring the blast on Crickley's distant steep.

Between the Boughs

Between the boughs the stars showed numberless
And the leaves were
As wonderful in blackness as those brightnesses
Hung in high air.

Two lovers in that whispering silence, what
Should fright our peace?
The aloofness, the dread of starry majesties,
The night-stilled trees.

If I Walked Straight Slap

If I walked straight slap
Headlong down the road
Toward the two-wood gap
Should I hit that cloud?

The Valley Farm

Ages ago the waters covered here
And took the light of dayspring as a mirror:
Hundreds of tiny spikes and threads of light.
But now the spikes are hawthorn, and the hedges
Are foamed like ocean's crests and peace waits here
Deeper than middle South Sea, or the Fortunate
Or fabled islands. And blue wood-smoke rising
Foretells smooth weather and the airs of peace.
Even the woodchopper swinging bright
His lithe and noble weapon in the sun,
Moves with such grace peace works an act through him,
Those echoes thud and leave a deeper peace.
If War should come here only then might one
Regret receding water and earth left
To bear man's grain and use his mind of order
Working to frame such squares and lights as these.

I Saw England – July Night

She was a village
Of lonely knowledge
The high roads left her aside, she was forlorn, a maid.
Water ran there, dusk hid her, she climbed four-wayed
Brown-golden windows showed last folk not yet asleep;
Water ran, was a centre of silence endless deep. . . .
Fathomless deeps of pricked sky, almost fathomless

Hollowed an upward gaze in pale satin of blue.
But I was happy indeed, outwards I got driven,
Yet despite all, given
A sign undoubtful of an England that few
Doubt, not many have seen,
That Will Squele he knew and so was shriven.
Home of Twelfth Night – Edward Thomas by Arras fallen,
Borrow and Hardy, Sussex tales out of Roman heights callen.
No madrigals or field-songs to my all reverent whim;
Till I got back I was dumb.

When March Blows

When March blows, and Monday's linen is shown
On the gooseberry bushes, and the worried washer alone
Fights at the soaked stuff; meres and the rutted pools
Mirror the wool-pack clouds and shine clearer than jewels.

And the children throw stones in them, spoil mirrors and clouds.
The worry of washing over; the worry of foods
Brings tea-time; March quietens as the trouble dies . . .
The washing is brought in under wind-swept clear infinite skies.

Yesterday Lost

What things I have missed today, I know very well,
But the seeing of them each new time is miracle.
Nothing between Bredon and Dursley has
Any day yesterday's precise unpraiséd grace.
The changed light, or curve changed mistily,
Coppice, now bold cut, yesterday's mystery.
A sense of mornings, once seen, for ever gone,
Its own for ever: alive, dead, and my possession.

The Lock Keeper

Men delight to praise men; and to edge
A little further off from death the memory
Of any noted or bright personality,
Is still a luck and poet's privilege.
And so the man who goes in my dark mind
With sand and broad waters and general kind
Of fish-and-fox-and-bird lore, and walking lank:
Knowledge of net and rod and rib and shank,
Might well stretch out my mind to be a frame –
A picture of a worthy without name.
You might see him at morning by the lock-gates,
Or busy in the warehouse on a multitude
Of boat fittings, net fittings; copper, iron, wood,
Then later digging, furious, electric
Under the apple boughs with a short stick,
Burnt black long ages, of pipe between set teeth,
His eyes gone flaming on the work beneath –
He up-and-down working like a marionette.
Back set, eyes set, wrists; and the work self-set.

His afternoon was action but all nebulous
Trailed over four miles country, tentaculous
Of coalmen, farmers, fishermen his friends,
And duties without beginnings and without ends.
There was talk with equals, there were birds and fish to
    observe,
Stuff for a hundred thoughts on the canal's curves,
A world of sight – and back in time for tea;
Or the tide's change, his care; or a barge to let free;
The lowering of the waters, the quick inflow,
The trouble and the turmoil; characteristic row
Of exits or of river entrances;
With old (how old?) cries of the straining crews,
(Norse, Phoenician, Norse, British? Immemorial use.)

Tins would float shining at three-quarter tide;
Midstream his line of fire, never far wide –
Dimples of water showed his aim a guide,
And ringed the sunset colours with bright ripples.

Later, tide being past violence, the gates known safe,
He would leave his station, lock warehouse and half
Conscious of tiredness now, moving lankly and slow,
Would go in a dark time like some phantom or wraith,
Most like a woodsman in full summer glow.
There he was not known to me, but as hearers know
Outside the blue door facing the canal path;
Two hours or three hours of talk; as the fishers know
Or sailors, or poachers, or wandering men know talk.

Poverty or closing time would bring him again.
On the cinder path outside would be heard his slow walk.
It had a width, that Severn chimney-corner,
A dignity and largeness which should make grave
Each word or cadence uttered or let fall, save
When the dark wind in garden shrubs was mourner.
It would have needed one far less sick than I
To have questioned, to have pried each vein of his wide lore.
One should be stable, and be able for wide views,
Have knowledge, and skilled manage of questions use
When the captain is met, the capable in use,
The pictured mind, the skilled one, the hawk-eyed one:
The deft-handed, quick-moving the touch-commanded one.

Man and element and animal comprehending
And all-paralleling one. His knowledge transcending
Books, from long vain searches of dull fact.
Conviction needing instant change to act.
The nights of winter netting birds in hedges;
The stalking wild-duck by down-river sedges;
The tricks of sailing; fashions of salmon-netting:
Cunning of practice, the finding, doing, the getting –

Wisdom of every various season or light –
Fish running, tide running, plant learning and bird flight.
Short cuts, and watercress beds, and all snaring touches,
Angling and line laying and wild beast brushes;
Badgers, stoats, foxes, the few snakes, care of ferrets,
Exactly known and judged of on their merits.
Bee-swarming, wasp-exterminating and bird-stuffing.

There was nothing he did not know; there was nothing, nothing.

Some men are best seen in the full day shine,
Some in half-light or the dark star-light fine:
But he, close in the deep chimney-corner seen
Shadow and bright flare, saturnine and lean;
Clouded with smoke, wrapped round with cloak of thought,
He gave more of desert to me – more than I ought –
Who was more used to book-poring than bright life.

One had seen half-height covering the stretched sand
With purpose, insistent, creeping-up with silver band,
But dark determined, making wide on and sure.
So behind talk flowed the true spirit to endure,
To perceive, to manage, to be skilled to excel, to comprehend;
A net of craft of eye, heart, kenning and hand.
Thousand-threaded tentaculous intellect
Not easy on a new thing to be wrecked –
Since cautious with ableness, and circumspect
In courage, his mind moved to a new stand,
And only with full wisdom used that hand.

Months of firelight and lamplight of night-times; before-bed
Revelations; time of learning and little said
On my part, since the master he was so wise –
Easy the lesson; while the grave night-winds' sighs

At window or up chimney incessant moaning
For dead daylight or for music or fishermen dead.
Dark river voice below heard and lock's overflow.

The Dearness of Common Things

The dearness of common things,
Beech wood, tea, plate shelves,
And the whole family of crockery,
Woodaxes, blades, helves.

Ivory milk, earth's coffee,
The white face of books
And the touch, feel, smell of paper,
Latin's lovely looks.

Earth fine to handle,
The touch of clouds
When the imagined arm leaps out to caress
Grey worsted or wool clouds.

Wool, rope, cloth, old pipes
Gone warped in service
And the one herb of tobacco,
The herb of grace, the censer weed
Of blue whorls, finger-traced curves –
The touch of sight how strange and marvellous
To any blind man pierced through his opaque,
When concrete objects grow.

Water Colours

The trembling water glimpsed through dark tangle
Of late-month April's delicatest thorn,
One moment put the cuckoo-flower to scorn
Where its head hangs by sedges, Severn bank-full.

But dark water has a hundred fires on it;
As the sky changes it changes and ranges through
Sky colours and thorn colours, and more would do,
Were not the blossom truth so quick on it,
And Beauty brief in action as first dew.

Laventie

One would remember still
Meadows and low hill
Laventie was, as to the line and elm row
Growing as green leaves wounded as home elms grow.
Shimmer of summer there and blue autumn mists
Seen from trench-ditch winding in mazy twists.
The Australian gunners in close flowery hiding
Cunning found out at last, and smashed in the unspeakable lists.
And the guns in the smashed wood thumping and griding.

The letters written there, and received there,
Books, cakes, cigarettes in a parish of famine
And leaks in rainy times with general damning.
The crater, and carrying of gas cylinders on two sticks
(Pain past comparison and far past right agony gone)
Strained hopelessly of heart and frame at first fix.

Café-au-lait in dug-outs on Tommies' cookers,
Cursed minnie werfs, and thirst in summer.
The Australian miners clayed, and the being afraid
Before strafes, sultry August dusk time than death dumber –
And the cooler hush after the strafe, and the long night wait –
The relief of first dawn, the crawling out to look at it,
Wonder divine of Dawn, man hesitating before Heaven's gate.

(Though not on Cooper's where music fire took at it.
Though not as at Framilode beauty where body did shake
at it.)
Yet the dawn with aeroplanes crawling high at Heaven
gate
Lovely aerial beetles of wonderful scintillate
Strangest interest, and puffs of soft purest white –
Soaking light, dispersing colouring for fancy's delight.

Of Machonachie, Paxton, Tickler and Stephens;
Fray Bentos, Spiller and Baker, odds and evens
Of trench food, but the everlasting craving
For bread, the pure thing, blessed beyond saving.
Canteen disappointments, and the keen boy braving
Bullets or such for grouse roused surprisingly through
(Halfway) Stand-to.
And the shell nearly blunted my razor at shaving,
Tilleloy, Fauquissart, Neuve Chapelle, and mud like glue.

But Laventie, most of all, I think is to soldiers
The town itself with plane trees, and small-spa air;
And vin rouge-blanc, chocolat, citron, grenadine:
One might buy in small delectable cafés there.
The broken church, and vegetable fields bare;
Neat French market town look so clean,
And the clarity, amiability of North French air.
Like water flowing beneath the dark plough and high
Heaven,
Music's delight to please the poet pack-marching there.

Half Dead

Half dead with sheer tiredness, wakened quick at night
With dysentery pangs, going blind among dim sleepers
And dazed into half dark, illness had its spite.
Head cleared, eyes saw; pangs and ill body-creepers

Stilled with the cold – the cold bringing me sane –
See there was Witcombe Steep as it were, but no beeches there.
Yet still clear flames of stars over the crest bare,
Mysterious glowing on the cloths of heaven.
Sirius or Mars or Argo's stars, and high the Sisters – the
Pleiads – those seven.

Best turn in, fatigue party out at seven. . . .
What though beauty was – I had been Cranham's walks. . . .
Dark was the billet after that seeing of rare
Gold stars, stumbling among the still forms to my lair.
Still were the stars bright – my sick mind hung on them even.

But long after: in solitary day walking I recalled
Caulaincourt's Mausoleum and the stars March midnight
called;
On the east horizon's dim loveliest shape upheld.
To mix with music in my thought and forget sickness –
To drown sorrow deep that on me was then masterless –
Hunger and weak body and tired of needed sleep.
For Argo or Sirius in the east skies or for Regulus.

Crucifix Corner

There was a water dump there and regimental
Carts came every day to line up and fill full
Those rolling tanks with chlorinated clay mixture
And curse the mud with vain veritable vexture.
Aveluy across the valley, billets, shacks, ruins.
With time and time a crump there to mark doings.
On New Year's Eve the marsh gloomed tremulous
With rosy mist still holding so marvellous
Sunglow; the air smelt home; the breathed home –
Noel not put away; New Year's Eve not yet come.
All things said 'Severn', the air was of those dusk meadows –
Transport rattled somewhere in southern shadows,

Stars that were not strange ruled the lit tranquil sky,
Arched far and high.

What should break that but gun-noise or Last Trump?
Neither broke it. Suddenly at a light jump
Clarinet sang into 'Hundred Pipers and A'' –
Aveluy's pipers answered with pipers' true call
'Happy we've been a-tegether' when nothing, nothing
Stayed of war-weariness or Winter-loathing.
Cracker with stockings hung in the quaint Heavens
Orion and the seven stars, comical at odds and evens –
Gaiety split discipline in sixes or sevens –
Hunger mixed strangely with magical leavens.
It was as if Cinderella had opened the Ball
And music put aside the time's saddened clothing.
It was as if Sir Walter were company again
In the late night – 'Antiquary' or 'Midlothian' –
Or 'Redgauntlet' bringing Solway clear to the mind.
After music, and a day of walking or making,
To return to music, or to read the starred dark dawn-blind.

Strange Hells

There are strange Hells within the minds War made
Not so often, not so humiliatingly afraid
As one would have expected – the racket and fear
    guns made.
One Hell the Gloucester soldiers they quite put out:
Their first bombardment, when in combined black shout
Of fury, guns aligned, they ducked lower their heads –
And sang with diaphragms fixed beyond all dreads,
That tin and stretched-wire tinkle, that blither of tune:
'Après la guerre fini', till Hell all had come down.
Twelve-inch, six-inch, and eighteen pounders hammering
    Hell's thunders.

Where are they now, on State-doles, or showing shop-patterns
Or walking town to town sore in borrowed tatterns
Or begged. Some civic routine one never learns.
The heart burns – but has to keep out of face how heart burns.

After War

One got peace of heart at last, the dark march over,
And the straps slipped, the warmth felt under roof's low
    cover,
Lying slack the body, let sink in straw giving;
And some sweetness, a great sweetness felt in mere living,
And to come to this haven after sorefooted weeks,
The dark barn roof, and the glows and the wedges and
    streaks;
Letters from home, dry warmth and still sure rest taken
Sweet to the chilled frame, nerves soothed were so sore
    shaken.

Near Vermand

Lying flat on my belly shivering in clutch-frost,
There was time to watch the stars, we had dug in:
Looking eastward over the low ridge; March scurried its blast
At our senses, no use either dying or struggling.
Low woods to left, Cotswold spinnies if ever,
Showed through snow flurries and the clearer star weather,
And nothing but chill and wonder lived in mind; nothing
But loathing and fine beauty, and wet loathed clothing.
Here were thoughts. Cold smothering and fire-desiring,
A day to follow like this or in digging or wiring.

Worry in snow flurry and lying flat, flesh the earth loathing.
I was the forward sentry and would be relieved
In a quarter or so, but nothing more better than to crouch
Low in the scraped holes and to have frozen and rocky couch –

To be by desperate home thoughts clutched at, and
heart-grieved.
Was I ever there – a lit warm room and Bach, to search out
sacred
Meaning; and to find no luck; and to take love as believed.

Early Spring Dawn

Long shines the thin light of the day to north-east,
The line of blue faint known and the leaping to white;
The meadows lighten, mists lessen, but light is increased,
The sun soon will appear, and dance leaping with light.

Now milkers hear faint through dreams first cockerel crow,
Faint yet arousing thought, soon must the milk pails be
flowing.
Gone out the level sheets of mists, and see, the West row
Of elms are black on the meadow edge. Day's wind is
blowing.

First Time In

After the dread tales and red yarns of the Line
Anything might have come to us; but the divine
Afterglow brought us up to a Welsh colony
Hiding in sandbag ditches, whispering consolatory
Soft foreign things. Then we were taken in
To low huts candle-lit, shaded close by slitten
Oilsheets, and there but boys gave us kind welcome,
So that we looked out as from the edge of home.
Sang us Welsh things, and changed all former notions
To human hopeful things. And the next day's guns
Nor any Line-pangs ever quite could blot out
That strangely beautiful entry to War's rout;
Candles they gave us, precious and shared over-rations –
Ulysses found little more in his wanderings without doubt.

'David of the White Rock', the 'Slumber Song' so soft, and that
Beautiful tune to which roguish words by Welsh pit boys
Are sung – but never more beautiful than here under the guns' noise.

Behind the Line

I suppose France this morning is as white as here
High white clouds veiling the sun, and the mere
Cabbage fields and potato plants lovely to see,
Back behind at Robecq there with the day free.

In the estaminets I suppose the air as cool, and the floor
Grateful dark red; the beer and the different store
Of citron, grenadine, red wine as surely delectable
As in Nineteen Sixteen; with the round stains on the dark table.

Journals Français tell the same news and the queer
Black printed columns give news, but no longer the fear
Of shrapnel or any evil metal torments.
High white morning as here one is sure is on France.

Old Dreams

Once I had dreamed of return to a sunlit land
Of summer and firelit winter with inns to visit,
But here are tangles of Fate one does not understand,
And as for rest or true ease, where is it or what is it.

With criss-cross purposes and spoilt threads of life,
Perverse pathways, the savour of life is gone.
What have I then with crumbling wood or glowing coals,
Or a four-hours' walking, to work, through a setting sun?

The Not-Returning

Never comes now the through-and-through clear
Tiredness of body on crisp straw down laid,
Nor the tired thing said
Content before the clean sleep close the eyes. . . .
Or ever resistless rise
Pictures of far country Westward, Westward out of sight
of the eyes.

Never more delights comes of the roof dark lit
With under-candle-flicker nor rich gloom on it,
The limned faces, and moving hands shuffling the cards,
The clear conscience, the free mind moving towards
Poetry, friends, music, the old earthly rewards.
No more they come – no more.
Only the restless searching, the bitter labour,
The going out to watch stars, stumbling blind through the
difficult door.

Towards Lillers

In October marching, taking the sweet air,
Packs riding lightly, and home-thoughts soft coming,
'This is right marching, we are even glad to be here,
Or very glad?' But looking upward to dark smoke
foaming,
Chimneys on the clear crest, no more shades for roaming,
Smoke covering sooty what man's heart holds dear,
Lillers we approached, a quench for thirsty frames,
And looked once more between houses and at queer names
Of estaminets, longed for cool wine or cold beer.
This was war; we understood; moving and shifting about;
To stand or be withstood in the mixéd rout
Of fight to come after this. But that was a good dream

Of justice or strength-test with steel tool a gleam
Made to the hand. But barb-wire lay to the front,
Tiny aeroplanes circled as ever their wont
High over the two ditches of heart-sick men;
The times scientific, as evil as ever, again.
October lovely bathing with sweet air the plain.

*

Gone outward to the east and the new skies
Are aeroplanes, and float there as tiny as bright
As insects wonderful coloured after the night
Emerging lovely as ever into the new day's
First coolness and lucent gratefulnesses
Of the absorbing wide praises of middle sight –
Men clean their rifles insentient at that delight;
Wonder increases as fast as the night dies.

Now up to the high above aeroplanes go
Swift bitter smoke puffs and spiteful flames,
None knows the pilots, none guesses at their names,
They fly unthought courses of common danger,
Honour rides on the frame with them through that anger,
As the heroes of Marathon their renown we know.

Sonnet – September 1922

Fierce indignation is best understood by those
Who have time or no fear, or a hope in its real good.
One loses it with a filed soul or in sentimental mood,
Anger is gone with sunset, or flows as flows
The water in easy mill-runs; the earth that ploughs
Forgets protestation in its turning, the rood
Prepares, considers, fulfils; and the poppy's blood
Makes old the old changing of the headland's brows.

But the toad under the harrow toadiness
Is known to forget, and even the butterfly
Has doubts of wisdom when that clanking thing
goes by
And's not distressed. A twisted thing keeps still
That thing easier twisted than a grocer's bill,
And no history of November keeps the guy.

The Incense Bearers

Toward the sun the drenched May-hedges lift
White rounded masses like still ocean-drift
And day fills with heavy scent of that gift.

There is no escaping that full current of thick
Incense; one walks, suddenly one comes quick
Into a flood of odour there, aromatic,

Not English; for cleaner, sweeter, is the hot scent that
Is given from hedges, solitary flowers, not
In mass, but lonely odours that scarcely float.

But the incense bearers, soakers of sun's full
Powerfulness, give out floods unchecked, wonderful
Utterance almost, which makes no poet grateful,

Since his love is for single things rarely found,
Or hardly. Violets blooming in remote ground.
One colour, one fragrance, like one uncompanied
sound –

Struck upon silence, nothing looked for, hung
As from gold wires, this May incense is swung,
Heavy of odour, the drenched meadows among.

To God

Why have you made life so intolerable
And set me between four walls, where I am able
Not to escape meals without prayer, for that is possible
Only by annoying an attendant. And tonight a sensual
Hell has been put on me, so that all has deserted me
And I am merely crying and trembling in heart
For Death, and cannot get it. And gone out is part
Of sanity. And there is dreadful Hell within me.
And nothing helps. Forced meals there have been and
electricity
And weakening of sanity by influence
That's dreadful to endure. And there is orders
And I am praying for death, death, death,
And dreadful is the in-drawing or out-breathing of breath,
Because of the intolerable insults put on my whole soul,
Of the soul loathed, loathed, loathed of the soul.
Gone out every bright thing from my mind.
All lost that ever God himself designed.
Not half can be written of cruelty of man, on man,
Not often such evil guessed as between Man and Man.

The Interview

Death I have often faced
In the damp trench – or poisoned waste:
Shell or shot, gas or flying steel, bayonet –
But only once by one bullet my arm was wet
With blood. Death faced me there, Death it was that I faced.
But now by no means may it come to me.
Mercy of Death noways vouchsafed to pain.
Were but those times of battle to come again!
Or even boat-sailing, danger on a mimic inland sea!
Death moaning, Death flying, shrieking in air.
Desiring its mark sufficient everywhere – everywhere.

Interview enough – but now I can not get near
Such challenge or dear enmity; pain more than fear
Oppresses me – Would that might come again!
Death in the narrow trench. . . . or wide in the fields.
Death in the Reserve, where the earth wild beautiful flowers
yields.
Death met – outfaced – but here: not to be got.
Prayed for, truly desired, obtainéd not –
A lot past dreadfulness, an unhuman lot.
For never Man was meant to be denied Chance
Of Ending pain past strength – O for France! For France!
Death walked freely one might be sought of him
Or seek, in twilight or first light of morning dim.
Death dreadful that scared the cheeks of blood,
Took friends, spoilt any happy true-human mood,
Shrieked in the near air threatened from upon high.
Dreadful, dreadful. But not to be come by
Now, confined no Interview is ever here.
And worse than Death is known in the spirit of fear.
Death is a thing desired, never to be had at all –
Spirit for Death cries, nothing hears; nothing granted here. O
If Mercy would but hear the cry of the spirit grow
From waking – till Death seems far beyond a right,
And dark is the spirit has all right to be bright.
Death is not here – save mercy grant it, when
Was cruelty such known last among like-and-like men?
An Interview? It is cried for – and not known –
Not found. Death absent what thing is truly Man's own?
Beaten down continually, continually beaten clean down.

Hedger

To me the A Major Concerto has been dearer
Than ever before, because I saw one weave
Wonderful patterns of bright green, never clearer
Of April; whose hand nothing at all did deceive –

Of laying right
The stakes of bright
Green lopped off spear-shaped, and stuck notched-
crooked up;
Wonder was quickened at workman's craftmanship
But clumsy were the efforts of my stiff body
To help him in the laying of bramble, ready
Of mind, but clumsy of muscle in helping. Rip
Of clothes unheeded. Torn hands, and his quick moving
Was never broken by any danger, his loving
Use of the bill or scythe was most deft, and clear –
Had my piano-playing or counterpoint
Been so without fear –
Then indeed fame had been mine of most bright outshining;
But never had I known singer or piano-player
So quick and sure in movement as this hedge-layer
This gap-mender, of quiet courage unhastening.

On Somme

Suddenly into the still air burst thudding
And thudding, and cold fear possessed me all,
On the gray slopes there, where Winter in sullen brooding
Hung between height and depth of the ugly fall
Of Heaven to earth; and the thudding was illness' own.
But still a hope I kept that were we there going over,
I, in the line, I should not fail, but take recover
From others' courage, and not as coward be known.
No flame we saw, the noise and the dread alone
Was battle to us; men were enduring there such
And such things, in wire tangled, to shatters blown.

Courage kept, but ready to vanish at first touch.
Fear, but just held. Poets were luckier once
In the hot fray swallowed and some magnificence.

After 'The Penny Whistle'

The heels hammered out in the frosty roadway
A rhythm long time not known
To a body and soul in long torment managed –
Winter and swiftness gone.

But at the Front there was such desiring,
Such hope in the going again,
With the telegraph wires singing frosty in January
Under stars friendly to men.

Those heels must stay still there, deep in frost mud,
While the imagination sought
To be back there, out of the agony, with shelter
To look to; and glowing fire caught

In bars of iron, with tea-kettle steaming,
And after a soak of blaze
And sauntering, preparing, music to be making
Of lovely lost unhappy days.

First Poem

O what will you turn out, book, to be?
Who are not my joy, but my escape from the worst
And most accurst of my woe? Shall you be poetry,
Or tell truth, or be of past things the tale rehearsed?

To Long Island First

To Long Island first with my tortured verse,
Remember how on a Gloucester book-stall one morning
I saw, brown 'Leaves of Grass' after long hesitation
(For fourpence to me was bankruptcy then or worse)

I bought, what since in book or mind about the dawning
On Roman Cotswold, Roman Artois war stations,
Severn and Buckingham, London after night wanderings,
Has served me, friend or Master on many occasions
Of weariness, or gloriousness or delight.
At first to puzzle, then grow past all traditions
To be Master unquestioned – a book that brings the clear
Spirit of him that wrote, to the thought again here.
If I have not known Long Island none has –
Brooklyn is my own City, Mannahattan the right of me,
Camden and Idaho – and all New England's
Two-fold love of honour, honour and homely grace.
If blood to blood can speak or the spirit has inspiring,
Let me claim place there also – Briton, I am also Hers,
And Roman; have more than Virgil for meditations.

Walt Whitman

With more knowledge of the poetic things, of the manly
things
But with no knowledge of Greek care in fashionings:
Forging out great thought like Beethoven, yet caught
In ignorance, not honouring makings of generations.
Not square to form of truth; thought to clear-of-thought
Always vowed – the maker, the companion of true kings,
(Whose page is coloured with earth's and his heart's blood).
Born of Paumanok, son of responding kisses,
Whom all the earth or sea surge desires or blesses;
Praised by Gloucesters in trench or marching mood
For his courage, colour or master-in-action mood:
(Bought of me just a hesitater in old Gloucester)
Never so much as now by me beloved, acknowledged.
What 'Song of Myself', or 'Drum Taps' or 'Brooklyn',
'Calamus', or 'Paumanok' strikes out or clean misses
Is best known by those who have to Death's face gone;
Or on a sentry post at last discovered 'This Compost' –
Shivering in March sleets, faithful in drearinesses.

Butchers and Tombs

After so much battering of fire and steel
It had seemed well to cover them with Cotswold stone –
And shortly praising their courage and quick skill
Leave them buried, hidden till the slow, inevitable
Change came should make them service of France alone.
But the times hurry, the commonness of the tale
Made it a thing not fitting ceremonial,
And so the disregarders of blister on heel,
Pack on shoulder, barrage and work at the wires,
One wooden cross had for ensign of honour and life
  gone –
Save when the Gloucesters turning sudden to tell to one
Some joke, would remember and say – 'That joke is done,'
Since he who would understand was so cold he could not
  feel,
And clay binds hard, and sandbags get rotten and crumble.

The Bohemians

Certain people would not clean their buttons,
Nor polish buckles after latest fashions,
Preferred their hair long, putties comfortable,
Barely escaping hanging, indeed hardly able;
In Bridge and smoking without army cautions
Spending hours that sped like evil for quickness,
(While others burnished brasses, earned promotions).
These were those ones who jested in the trench,
While others argued of army ways, and wrenched
What little soul they had still further from shape,
And died off one by one, or became officers
Without the first of dream, the ghost of notions
Of ever becoming soldiers, or smart and neat,
Surprised as ever to find the army capable

Of sounding, 'Lights out' to break a game of Bridge,
As to fear candles would set a barn alight:
In Artois or Picardy they lie – free of useless fashions.

The Silent One

Who died on the wires, and hung there, one of two –
Who for his hours of life had chattered through
Infinite lovely chatter of Bucks accent;
Yet faced unbroken wires; stepped over, and went,
A noble fool, faithful to his stripes – and ended.
But I weak, hungry, and willing only for the chance
Of line – to fight in the line, lay down under unbroken
Wires, and saw the flashes, and kept unshaken.
Till the politest voice – a finicking accent, said:
'Do you think you might crawl through, there: there's a hole?' In the afraid
Darkness, shot at; I smiled, as politely replied –
'I'm afraid not, Sir.' There was no hole, no way to be seen.
Nothing but chance of death, after tearing of clothes
Kept flat, and watched the darkness, hearing bullets whizzing –
And thought of music and swore deep heart's deep oaths
(Polite to God –) and retreated and came on again.
Again retreated – and a second time faced the screen.

War Books

What did they expect of our toil and extreme
Hunger – the perfect drawing of a heart's dream?
Did they look for a book of wrought art's perfection,
Who promised no reading, nor praise, nor publication?
Out of the heart's sickness the spirit wrote.
For delight, or to escape hunger, or of war's worst anger,
When the guns died to silence, and men would gather sense
Somehow together, and find this was life indeed.

And praise another's nobleness, or to Cotswold get hence.
There we wrote – Corbie Ridge – or in Gonnehem at rest.
Or Fauquissart or world's death songs, ever the best.
One made sorrows' praise passing the church where silence
Opened for the long quivering strokes of the bell –
Another wrote all soldiers' praise, and of France, and night's
stars –
Served his guns, got immortality, and died well.
But Ypres played another trick with its danger on me,
Kept still the needing and loving-of-action body;
Gave no candles, and nearly killed me twice as well.
And no souvenirs, though I risked my life in the stuck Tanks.
Yet there was praise of Ypres, love came sweet in hospital –
And old Flanders went under to long ages of plough thought
in my pages.

The Mangel-bury

It was after war, Edward Thomas had fallen at Arras –
I was walking by Gloucester musing on such things
As fill his verse with goodness; it was February; the long
house
Straw-thatched of the mangels stretched two wide wings;
And looked as part of the earth heaped up by dead soldiers
In the most fitting place – along the hedge's yet-bare lines.
West-spring breathed there early, that none foreign divines.
Across the flat country the rattling of the cart sounded:
Heavy of wood, jingling of iron; as he neared me, I waited
For the chance perhaps of heaving at those great rounded
Ruddy or orange things – and right to be rolled and hefted
By a body like mine, soldier-still, and clean from water.
Silent he assented; till the cart was drifted
High with those creatures, so right in size and matter,
We threw with our bodies swinging; blood in my ears
singing;
His was the thick-set sort of farmer, but well built –

Perhaps long before his blood's name ruled all:
Watched all things for his own. If my luck had so willed
Many questions of lordship I had heard him tell – old
Names, rumours. But my pain to more moving called
And him to some barn business far in the fifteen acre field.

Farewell

What! to have had gas, and to expect
No more than a week's sick, and to get Blighty –
This is the gods' gift, and not anyway exact –
To Ypres, or bad St Julien or Somme Farm.
Don Hancocks, shall I no more see your face frore,
Gloucester-good, in the first light? (But you are dead!)
Shall I see no more Monger with india-rubber
Twisted face? (But machine-gun caught him and his
grimace.)
No more to march happy with such good comrades,
Watching the sky, the brown land, the bayonet blades
Moving – to muse on music forgetting the pack.
Nor to hear Gloucester with Stroud debating the lack
Of goodliness or virtue in girls or farmlands.
Nor to hear Cheltenham hurling at Cotswold demands
Of civilization; nor West Severn joking at East Severn?
No more – across the azure and the brown lands
The morning mist or high day clear of rack
Shall move my dear knees – or feel them frosted, shivering
By Somme or Aubers – or to have a courage from faces
Full of all West England, Her God-given graces.
There was not one of all that Battalion
Loved his comrades as well as I – but kept shy.
Or said in verse, what his voice would not rehearse.
So, gassed, I went back – to Northlands where voices
speak soft as in verse.
And, after, to meet evil not fit for the thought one touch to
dwell on.

Dear Battalion, the dead of you would not have let
Your comrade be so long prey for the unquiet
Black evil of the unspoken and concealed pit.
You would have had me safe – dead or free happy alive.

They bruise my head and torture with their own past-hate
Sins of the past, and lie so as earth moves at it –
You dead ones – I lay with you under the unbroken wires once.

It is Near Toussaints

It is near Toussaints, the living and dead will say:
'Have they ended it? What has happened to Gurney?'
And along the leaf-strewed roads of France many brown
 shades
Will go, recalling singing, and a comrade for whom also they
Had hoped well. His honour them had happier made.
Curse all that hates good. When I spoke of my breaking
(Not understood) in London, they imagined of the taking
Vengeance, and seeing things were different in future.
(A musician was a cheap, honourable and nice creature.)
Kept sympathetic silence; heard their packs creaking
And burst into song – Hilaire Belloc was all our Master.
On the night of all the dead, they will remember me,
Pray Michael, Nicholas, Maries lost in Novembery
River-mist in the old City of our dear love, and batter
At doors about the farms crying 'Our war poet is lost',
'Madame – no bon!' – and cry his two names, warningly,
 somberly.

An Appeal for Death

There is one who all day wishes to die,
And appeals for it – without a reason why –
Since Death is easy if men are merciful.
Water and land with chances are packed full.

Who all day wishes to die. How many ages
Have denied Death – so who reads old-written pages
And finds 'This man suffered and prayed for Death,
And went beyond this, Desire of Life beneath.'
Bitterly, bitterly, and though he feels his wrongs,
And once took pride in verse-making and in songs,
Yet now, yet now would wish to rest, and be
Out of Pain, out of Life, quietly, as quietly
As pained men ever were meant to rest.
Humanity knows Earth to have as quiet a breast
As ever Mother's to a longing child.
Therefore in mercy let rest, let rest this wild
Or show hard torment, or of fear of such
Let rest, out of the fear of any pain's touch.
If men will not honour, nor find employ,
Will common mercy not forget what was wrong,
Remember what was good – a maker of Song
Asks, desires, has prayed for Mercy of Death
To end all, lie still – quiet green turf beneath,
Since promises forgotten are, and friendliness
Between so many men and him. The address
Of courtesy to casual wayfarers,
Small presents, courtesy of peace and wars –
To rest from pain, to trouble no one more –
Under green turf-mound, or by friendly shore
That will with rocking water lull his peace
That cannot now find hope nor strength nor ease.
To be let rest in mercy – to know an end
Of surety, Death's quiet surest of friend,
And what men would not, let calm Nature mend.

Hell's Prayer

My God, the wind is rising! on those edges
Of Cotswold dark glory might swing my soul –
And Western Severn and North of water sedges
Mystery sounds, the wind's drums roll.

None will care to walk there. Those prefer to tell
Tales in a warm room of gossips, gettings, wages,
While I would be cursing exultant at the wind's toll
Of bell, shout of glory – swiftness of shadows.
My birth, my earning, my attained heritages,
Ninety times denied me now thrust so far in hell.

I think of the gods, all their old oaths and gages –
Gloucester has clear honour sworn without fail –
Companionship of meadows, high Cotswold ledges
Battered now tonight with huge wind-bursts and rages,
Flying moon glimpses like a shattered and flimsy sail –
In Hell I buried a score-depth, writing verse pages.

December 30th

It is the year's end, the winds are blasting, and I
Write to keep madness and black torture away
A little – it is a hurt to my head not to complain.
In the world's places that honour earth, all men are thinking
Of centuries: all men of the ages of living and drinking;
Singing and company of all time till now –
(When the hate of Hell has this England's state plain).
By the places I know this night all the woods are battering
With the great blast, clouds fly low, and the moon
(If there is any) clamorous, dramatic, outspoken.

In such nights as this Lassington has been broken,
Severn flooded too high and banks overflown –
And the great words of 'Lear' first tonight have been spoken.
The boys of the villages growing up will say, 'I
Shall leave school, or have high wages, before another January –
Be grown up or free before again December's dark reign

Brights to Christmas, dies for the old year's memory.'
May to them the gods make not all prayers vain.

Cotswold edge, Severn Valley that watches two
Magnificences: noble at right times or affectionate,
What power of these gods ever now call to you
For the folks in you of right noble; and of delight
In all nature's things brought round in the year's circle?
Pray God in blastings, supplicate now in terrifical
Tempestuous movings about the high-sided night.

Men I have known fine, are dead in France, in exile,
One my friend is dumb, other friends dead also,
And I that loved you, past the soul am in torture's spite
Cursing the hour that bore me, pain that bred all
My greater longings; Love only to you, this last-year date.

Poem for End

So the last poem is laid flat in its place,
And Crickley with Crucifix Corner leaves from my face
Elizabethans and night-working thoughts – of such grace.

And all the dawns that set my thoughts new to making;
Or Crickley dusk that the beech leaves stirred to shaking
Are put aside – there is a book ended; heart aching.

Joy and sorrow, and all thoughts a poet thinks,
Walking or turning to music; the wrought-out links
Of fancy to fancy – by Severn or by Artois brinks.

Only what's false in this, blood itself would not save,
Sweat would not heighten – the dead Master in his grave
Would my true following of him, my care approve.

And more than he, I paid the prices of life
Standing where Rome immortal heard October's strife,
A war poet whose right of honour cuts falsehood like a
knife.

War poet – his right is of nobler steel – the careful sword –
And night walker will not suffer of praise the word
From the sleepers, the custom-followers, the dead lives
unstirred.

Only, who thought of England as two thousand years
Must keep of today's life the proper anger and fears:
England that was paid for by building and ploughing and
tears.

ISAAC ROSENBERG

Ode to David's Harp

Awake! ye joyful strains, awake!
In silence sleep no more;
Disperse the gloom that ever lies
O'er Judah's barren shore;
Where are the hands that strung thy chords
With tender touch and true,
Whose silvery tone impassioned all?
Those hands are silenced too.

Those chords whose tender strains awoke
In hearts that throbbed for war,
The martial stir when glory calls,
Lies mute on Judah's shore.
One chord awake – one strain prolong,
To wake the zeal in Israel's breast,
O sacred lyre once more how long?
'Tis vain – alas in silence rest.

Many a minstrel fame's elated
Envies thee thy harp and fame.
Harp of David – monarch minstrel
Bravely – bravely keep thy name.
Ay! every ear that listened
Was charmed – was thrilled – was bound,
Every eye with moisture glistened,
Thrilling to the harp's sweet sound.

Hark – the harp is pouring
Notes of burning fire,
And each soul o'erpowering
Melts the rousing ire,
Fiercer – shriller – wilder far
Than the brazen notes of war.

Accents sweet and echoes sweeter
Minstrel – minstrel, steeds fly fleeter,
Spurred on by thy magic strains,
Breasts are heaving – fate is weaving
Other bonds than slav'ry's chains,
For her chosen's blood are frozen
Icy fear in all their veins.

Tell me not the harp lies sleeping
Set not thus my heart aweeping,
In the muse's fairy dwelling
There thy magic notes are swelling.
But for list'ning mortals' ear
Vainly wait ye will not hear.
The chords are rent – for years have bent
Its living strings asunder.
But harp and name – shall life proclaim
In living voice of thunder.

Raphael

Dear, I have done; it shall be done. I know
I can paint on and on, and still paint on.
Another touch, and yet another touch.
Yet wherefore? 'Tis Art's triumph to know this,
Long ere the soul and brain begins to flag,
And dim the first fresh flashes of the soul,
Before achievement, by our own desire
And loathing to desist in what we love,
Is wrought to ruin by much overtoil,
To know the very moment of our gain,
And fix the triumph with reluctant pause.
Come from the throne, sweet, kiss me on the cheek;
You have borne bravely, sweet, come, look with me.
Is it not well – think love – the recompense,
This binds the unborn ages at our feet.
Thus you shall look, my love, and never change

Throughout all changes. Time's own conqueror,
While worshippers of climes and times unknown
Lingeringly look in wonder – here – at us.

What have we done – in these long hours, my love.
Long – long to you – whose patient labour was
To sit, and sit, a statue, movelessly.
Love we have woven a chain more glorious
Than crowns or Popes – to bind the centuries.
You are tired. I should have thought a little,
But you said nothing, sweet, and I forgot,
In rapture of my soul's imaginings.
You, – yes, 'twas thus you looked, ah, look again
That hint of smile – it was like wings for heaven,
And gave my spirit play to revel more
In dazzling visions. But ah! it mocked my hand.
There, – there – before my eyes and in my brain
Limned perfect – but my fingers traitors were,
Could not translate, and heartsick was the strife.
But it is done – I know not how – perchance
Even as I, maddened, drew on hopelessly
An angel taking pity – mayhap for thee –
Guided my hand and drew it easily.

And they will throng – admire with gaping mouth,
The students, 'Look, what ease, what grace divine.
What balance and what harmony serene'.
And some, 'Like noonday lakes to torrents wild,
After titanic Mighty Angelo.'
Ah, Angelo, he has no sweetness – true;
But, ah, I would I had his breadth of wing.
Jove's Thunders, and the giant craggy heights
Whose points cleave the high heavens, and at whose feet
The topmost clouds have end, afraid to soar.

And I too, shake my brow amongst the stars.
And this I know and feel what I have done
Is but the seed plot of a mightier world.

Yea, world on world is forming in my brain.
I have no space to hold it. Time will show
I could draw down the Heavens, I could bend
Yon hoar age-scorning column with my hand
I feel such power. But where there's sun, there's shade!
And these thoughts bring their shadow in their train.
Who lives? – See this, it is my hand – my name.
But who looks from the canvas, no – not me.
Some doubt of God – but the world lives who doubts?
Even thus our own creations mock at us,
Our own creations outlive our decay.

What do I labour for if all is thus.
I triumph, but my triumph is my scorn.
'Tis true I love my labour, and the days
Pass pleasantly,
But what is it I love in it – desire
Accomplished? never have I reached
The halfway of the purpose I have planned.
A hardship conquered? – a poor juggler's feat
And his elatement mayhap betters mine.
The adoration of the gaping crowd,
Who praise, with jest, not knowing why they praise,
Then turn, and sing a lewd and smutty song.
Or kneel – bate breath – to my Lord Cardinal.
Or is it the approval of the wise?
I take it – sadly knowing what I know,
And feeling that this marvel of their world
Is little triumph to me, it being my world;
Their deeds being circumscribed – proportionate,
Within their limits; and mine loftier,
But (God how bounded yet,) to do as thus
Is but my nature – therefore little pride
Their praises give me. Ah, but this gives pride
To know that there is one that does feel pride
When they praise me, and cannot hide the glow
Upon her cheeks to hear me spoken of.

Love – this is better – here – to be with you,
My head upon your bosom while your hair
A loosened fire falls all about my face
And thro' its tangles – like a prison bar
To shut my soul in – watch the shadows creep,
The long grey shadows creeping furtively.
I would I were a poet – love – this once.
I cannot tell my feelings . . .
How effable in this half-light you look,
Love I would dream – the shadows thickly press.
You fade into my fancy – and become
A thought – a smile – a rapture of the brain,
A presence that embraces all things felt.
A twilight glamour – faery fantasy.
Your two eyes in the shadow, stars that dream
In quiet waters of the evening, draw
My spirit to them and enfold me there
Love. I would sleep, dear love I would forget.
Love I would sleep, you watching, covering me,
Warmed by your love and sheltered 'neath love's wing,
Sweet let the world pass as this day has passed,
What do you murmur – sleeping? then will I.

Dust Calleth to Dust

A little dust whispered – a little grey dust,
As it whirled round my knees in the arms of the wind,
'O wind lift me higher, sweet wind, lift me higher
To see thro' his eyes to the vast of his mind'.

Then I soon heard it murmur – 'O brother, dear brother
How long must you guard that fierce temple of God?
So fixt to the earth and a foe to the wind –
O haste and with me kiss the cloud and the clod.'

On Receiving News of the War: Cape Town

Snow is a strange white word.
No ice or frost
Have asked of bud or bird
For Winter's cost.

Yet ice and frost and snow
From earth to sky
This Summer land doth know.
No man knows why.

In all men's hearts it is.
Some spirit old
Hath turned with malign kiss
Our lives to mould.

Red fangs have torn His face.
God's blood is shed.
He mourns from His lone place
His children dead.

O! ancient crimson curse!
Corrode, consume.
Give back this universe
Its pristine bloom.

The Dead Heroes

Flame out, you glorious skies,
Welcome our brave,
Kiss their exultant eyes;
Give what they gave.

Flash, mailèd seraphim,
Your burning spears;
New days to outflame their dim
Heroic years.

Thrills their baptismal tread
The bright proud air;
The embattled plumes outspread
Burn upwards there.

Flame out, flame out, O Song!
Star ring to star,
Strong as our hurt is strong
Our children are.

Their blood is England's heart;
By their dead hands
It is their noble part
That England stands.

England – Time gave them thee;
They gave back this
To win Eternity
And claim God's kiss.

At Sea-Point

Let the earth crumble away,
The heavens fade like a breath,
The sea go up in a cloud,
And its hills be given to death.

For the roots of the earth are old,
And the pillars of heaven are tired.
The hands that the sea enfold
Hath seen a new desired.

All things upon my sense
Are wasted spaces dull
Since one shape passed like a song
Let God all things annul.

A lie with its heart hidden
Is that cruel wall of air
That held her there unbidden,
Who comes not at my prayer.

Gone, who yet never came.
There is the breathing sea,
And the shining skies are the same,
But they lie – they lie to me.

For she stood with the sea below,
Between the sky and the sea,
She flew ere my soul was aware,
But left this thirst in me.

God Made Blind

It were a proud God-guiling, to allure
And flatter, by some cheat of ill, our Fate
To hold back the perfect crookedness, its hate
Devised, and keep it poor,
And ignorant of our joy, –
Masqued in a giant wrong of cruel annoy,
That stands as some bleak hut to frost and night,
While hidden in bed is warmth and mad delight.

For all Love's heady valour and loved pain
Towers in our sinews that may not suppress
(Shut to God's eye) Love's springing eagerness,

And mind to advance his gain
Of gleeful secrecy
Through dolorous clay, which his eternity
Has pierced, in light that pushes out to meet
Eternity without us, heaven's heat.

And then, when Love's power hath increased so
That we must burst or grow to give it room,
And we can no more cheat our God with gloom,
We'll cheat Him with our joy.
For say! what can God do
To us, to Love, whom we have grown into?
Love! the poured rays of God's Eternity!
We are grown God – and shall His self-hate be?

The Blind God

Streaked with immortal blasphemies
Betwixt His twin eternities
Shaper of mortal destinies
Sits in that limbo of dreamless sleep,
Some nothing that hath shadows deep.

The world is only a small pool
In the meadows of Eternity
And the wise man and the fool
In its depths like fishes lie,
When an angel drops a rod
And he draws you to the sky
Will you bear to meet your God
You have streaked with blasphemy?

Wedded [II]

They leave their love-lorn haunts,
Their sigh-warm floating Eden;
And they are mute at once;
Mortals, by God unheeden;
By their past kisses chidden.

But they have kist and known
Clear things we dim by guesses; –
Spirit to spirit grown: –
Heaven, born in hand caresses: –
Love, fall from sheltering tresses.

And they are dumb and strange;
Bared trees bowed from each other.
Their last green interchange
What lost dreams shall discover?
Dead, strayed, to love-stranged lover.

God

In his malodorous brain what slugs and mire
Lanthorned in his oblique eyes, guttering burned!
His body lodged a rat where men nursed souls.
The world flashed grape-green eyes of a foiled cat
To him. On fragments of a skull of power,
On shy and maimed, on women wrung awry,
He lay, a bullying hulk, to crush them more.
But when one, fearless, turned and clawed like bronze,
Cringing was easy to blunt these stern paws,
And he would weigh the heavier on those after.

Who rests in God's mean flattery now? Your wealth
Is but his cunning to make death more hard.
Your iron sinews take more pain in breaking.
And he has made the market for your beauty
Too poor to buy, although you die to sell.

Only that he has never heard of sleep;
And when the cats come out the rats are sly.
Here we are safe till he slinks in at dawn.

But he has gnawed a fibre from strange roots,
And in the morning some pale wonder ceases.
Things are not strange and strange things are forgetful.
Ah! if the day were arid, somehow lost,
Out of us, but it is as hair of us,
And only in the hush no wind stirs it.
And in the light vague trouble lifts and breathes,
And restlessness still shadows the lost ways.
The fingers shut on voices that pass through,
Where blind farewells are taken easily.

Ah! this miasma of a rotting God!

Marching – as seen from the left file

My eyes catch ruddy necks
Sturdily pressed back, –
All a red brick moving glint.
Like flaming pendulums, hands
Swing across the khaki –
Mustard-coloured khaki –
To the automatic feet.

We husband the ancient glory
In these bared necks and hands.
Not broke is the forge of Mars;
But a subtler brain beats iron

To shoe the hoofs of death,
(Who paws dynamic air now).
Blind fingers loose an iron cloud
To rain immortal darkness
On strong eyes.

'A worm fed on the heart of Corinth'

A worm fed on the heart of Corinth,
Babylon and Rome.
Not Paris raped tall Helen,
But this incestuous worm
Who lured her vivid beauty
To his amorphous sleep.
England! famous as Helen
Is thy betrothal sung.
To him the shadowless,
More amorous than Solomon.

In the Trenches

I snatched two poppies
From the parapet's edge,
Two bright red poppies
That winked on the ledge.
Behind my ear
I stuck one through,
One blood red poppy
I gave to you.

The sandbags narrowed
And screwed out our jest,
And tore the poppy
You had on your breast . . .

Down – a shell – O! Christ.
I am choked . . . safe . . . dust blind – I
See trench floor poppies
Strewn. Smashed you lie.

Break of Day in the Trenches

The darkness crumbles away.
It is the same old Druid Time as ever.
Only a live thing leaps my hand,
A queer sardonic rat,
As I pull the parapet's poppy
To stick behind my ear.
Droll rat, they would shoot you if they knew
Your cosmopolitan sympathies.
Now you have touched this English hand
You will do the same to a German
Soon, no doubt, if it be your pleasure
To cross the sleeping green between.
It seems, odd thing, you grin as you pass
Strong eyes, fine limbs, haughty athletes,
Less chanced than you for life,
Bonds to the whims of murder,
Sprawled in the bowels of the earth,
The torn fields of France.
What do you see in our eyes
At the shrieking iron and flame
Hurl'd through still heavens?
What quaver – what heart aghast?
Poppies whose roots are in man's veins
Drop, and are ever dropping,
But mine in my ear is safe –
Just a little white with the dust.

August 1914

What in our lives is burnt
In the fire of this?
The heart's dear granary?
The much we shall miss?

Three lives hath one life –
Iron, honey, gold.
The gold, the honey gone –
Left is the hard and cold.

Iron are our lives
Molten right through our youth.
A burnt space through ripe fields,
A fair mouth's broken tooth.

The Dying Soldier

'Here are houses' he moaned,
'I could reach but my brain swims.'
Then they thundered and flashed
And shook the earth to its rims.

'They are gunpits' he gasped,
'Our men are at the guns.
Water . . . Water . . . O water
For one of England's dying sons.'

'We cannot give you water,
Were all England in your breath.'
'Water! . . . Water! . . . O! Water!'
He moaned and swooned to death.

The Immortals

I killed them but they would not die.
Yea! all the day and all the night
For them I could not rest or sleep,
Nor guard from them nor hide in flight.

Then in my agony I turned
And made my hands red in their gore.
In vain – for faster than I slew
They rose more cruel than before.

I killed and killed with slaughter mad;
I killed till all my strength was gone.
And still they rose to torture me
For Devils only die in fun.

I used to think the devil hid
In women's smiles and wine's carouse.
I called him Satan, Balzebub.
But now I call him, dirty louse.

Louse Hunting

Nudes – stark aglisten
Yelling in lurid glee. Grinning faces of fiends
And raging limbs
Whirl over the floor one fire,
For a shirt verminously busy
Yon soldier tore from his throat
With oaths
Godhead might shrink at, but not the lice.
And soon the shirt was aflare
Over the candle he'd lit while we lay.

Then we all sprung up and stript
To hunt the vermin brood.
Soon like a demons' pantomime
The place was raging.
See the silhouettes agape,
See the gibbering shadows
Mixed with the battled arms on the wall.
See gargantuan hooked fingers
Dug in supreme flesh
To smutch the supreme littleness.
See the merry limbs in hot Highland fling
Because some wizard vermin
Charmed from the quiet this revel
When our ears were half lulled
By the dark music
Blown from Sleep's trumpet.

From France

The spirit drank the Café lights;
All the hot life that glittered there,
And heard men say to women gay,
'Life is just so in France'.

The spirit dreams of Café lights,
And golden faces and soft tones,
And hears men groan to broken men,
'This is not Life in France'.

Heaped stones and a charred signboard shows
With grass between and dead folk under,
And some birds sing, while the spirit takes wing.
And this is life in France.

Returning, we hear the larks

Sombre the night is.
And though we have our lives, we know
What sinister threat lurks there.

Dragging these anguished limbs, we only know
This poison-blasted track opens on our camp –
On a little safe sleep.

But hark! joy – joy – strange joy.
Lo! heights of night ringing with unseen larks.
Music showering our upturned list'ning faces.

Death could drop from the dark
As easily as song –
But song only dropped,
Like a blind man's dreams on the sand
By dangerous tides,
Like a girl's dark hair for she dreams no ruin lies there,
Or her kisses where a serpent hides.

Dead Man's Dump

The plunging limbers over the shattered track
Racketed with their rusty freight,
Stuck out like many crowns of thorns,
And the rusty stakes like sceptres old
To stay the flood of brutish men
Upon our brothers dear.

The wheels lurched over sprawled dead
But pained them not, though their bones crunched,
Their shut mouths made no moan,
They lie there huddled, friend and foeman,

Man born of man, and born of woman,
And shells go crying over them
From night till night and now.

Earth has waited for them
All the time of their growth
Fretting for their decay:
Now she has them at last!
In the strength of their strength
Suspended – stopped and held.

What fierce imaginings their dark souls lit
Earth! have they gone into you?
Somewhere they must have gone,
And flung on your hard back
Is their soul's sack,
Emptied of God-ancestralled essences.
Who hurled them out? Who hurled?

None saw their spirits' shadow shake the grass,
Or stood aside for the half used life to pass
Out of those doomed nostrils and the doomed mouth,
When the swift iron burning bee
Drained the wild honey of their youth.

What of us, who flung on the shrieking pyre,
Walk, our usual thoughts untouched,
Our lucky limbs as on ichor fed,
Immortal seeming ever?
Perhaps when the flames beat loud on us,
A fear may choke in our veins
And the startled blood may stop.

The air is loud with death,
The dark air spurts with fire
The explosions ceaseless are.

Timelessly now, some minutes past,
These dead strode time with vigorous life,
Till the shrapnel called 'an end!'
But not to all. In bleeding pangs
Some borne on stretchers dreamed of home,
Dear things, war-blotted from their hearts.

A man's brains splattered on
A stretcher-bearer's face;
His shook shoulders slipped their load,
But when they bent to look again
The drowning soul was sunk too deep
For human tenderness.

They left this dead with the older dead,
Stretched at the cross roads.

Burnt black by strange decay
Their sinister faces lie
The lid over each eye,
The grass and coloured clay
More motion have than they,
Joined to the great sunk silences.

Here is one not long dead;
His dark hearing caught our far wheels,
And the choked soul stretched weak hands
To reach the living word the far wheels said,
The blood-dazed intelligence beating for light,
Crying through the suspense of the far torturing wheels
Swift for the end to break,
Or the wheels to break,
Cried as the tide of the world broke over his sight.

Will they come? Will they ever come?
Even as the mixed hoofs of the mules,
The quivering-bellied mules,

And the rushing wheels all mixed
With his tortured upturned sight,
So we crashed round the bend,
We heard his weak scream,
We heard his very last sound,
And our wheels grazed his dead face.

Daughters of War

Space beats the ruddy freedom of their limbs –
Their naked dances with man's spirit naked
By the root side of the tree of life
(The underside of things
And shut from earth's profoundest eyes).

I saw in prophetic gleams
These mighty daughters in their dances
Beckon each soul aghast from its crimson corpse
To mix in their glittering dances.
I heard the mighty daughters' giant sighs
In sleepless passion for the sons of valour,
And envy of the days of flesh
Barring their love with mortal boughs across, –
The mortal boughs – the mortal tree of life,
The old bark burnt with iron wars
They blow to a live flame
To char the young green days
And reach the occult soul; – they have no softer lure –
No softer lure than the savage ways of death.
We were satisfied of our Lords the moon and the sun
To take our wage of sleep and bread and warmth –
These maidens came – these strong everliving Amazons,
And in an easy might their wrists
Of night's sway and noon's sway the sceptres brake,
Clouding the wild – the soft lustres of our eyes.

Clouding the wild lustres, the clinging tender lights;
Driving the darkness into the flame of day,
With the Amazonian wind of them
Over our corroding faces
That must be broken – broken for evermore
So the soul can leap out
Into their huge embraces.
Tho' there are human faces
Best sculptures of Deity,
And sinews lusted after
By the Archangels tall,
Even these must leap to the love-heat of these maidens
From the flame of terrene days,
Leaving grey ashes to the wind – to the wind.

One (whose great lifted face,
Where wisdom's strength and beauty's strength
And the thewed strength of large beasts
Moved and merged, gloomed and lit)
Was speaking, surely, as the earth-men's earth fell away;
Whose new hearing drunk the sound
Where pictures lutes and mountains mixed
With the loosed spirit of a thought,
Essenced to language, thus –

'My sisters force their males
From the doomed earth, from the doomed glee
And hankering of hearts.
Frail hands gleam up through the human quagmire,
    and lips of ash
Seem to wait, as in sad faded paintings
Far sunken and strange.
My sisters have their males
Clean of the dust of old days
That clings about those white hands,

And yearns in those voices sad.
But these shall not see them,
Or think of them in any days or years,
They are my sisters' lovers in other days and years.'

The Jew

Moses, from whose loins I sprung,
Lit by a lamp in his blood
Ten immutable rules, a moon
For mutable lampless men.

The blonde, the bronze, the ruddy,
With the same heaving blood,
Keep tide to the moon of Moses,
Then why do they sneer at me?

Girl to Soldier on Leave

I love you – Titan lover,
My own storm-days' Titan.
Greater than the son of Zeus.
I know who I would choose.

Titan – my splendid rebel –
The old Prometheus
Wanes like a ghost before your power –
His pangs were joys to yours.

Pallid days arid and wan
Tied your soul fast.
Babel cities' smoky tops
Pressed upon your growth

Weary gyves. What were you?
But a word in the brain's ways,
Or the sleep of Circe's swine.
One gyve holds you yet. –

It held you hiddenly on the Somme
Tied from my heart at home.
O must it loosen now? – I wish
You were bound with the old old gyves.

Love! you love me – your eyes
Have looked through death at mine.
You have tempted a grave too much.
I let you – I repine.

Soldier: Twentieth Century

I love you, great new Titan!
Am I not you?
Napoleon and Caesar
Out of you grew.

Out of unthinkable torture,
Eyes kissed by death,
Won back to the world again,
Lost and won in a breath,

Cruel men are made immortal.
Out of your pain born.
They have stolen the sun's power
With their feet on your shoulders worn.

Let them shrink from your girth,
That has outgrown the pallid days,
When you slept like Circe's swine,
Or a word in the brain's ways.

'Through these pale cold days'

Through these pale cold days
What dark faces burn
Out of three thousand years,
And their wild eyes yearn,

While underneath their brows
Like waifs their spirits grope
For the pools of Hebron again
For Lebanon's summer slope.

They leave these blond still days
In dust behind their tread
They see with living eyes
How long they have been dead.

WILFRED OWEN

Uriconium
An Ode

It lieth low near merry England's heart
Like a long-buried sin; and Englishmen
Forget that in its death their sires had part.
And, like a sin, Time lays it bare again
 To tell of races wronged,
And ancient glories suddenly overcast,
And treasures flung to fire and rabble wrath.
 If thou hast ever longed
To lift the gloomy curtain of Time Past,
And spy the secret things that Hades hath,
Here through this riven ground take such a view.
The dust, that fell unnoted as a dew,
Wrapped the dead city's face like mummy-cloth:
All is as was: except for worm and moth.

Since Jove was worshipped under Wrekin's shade
Or Latin phrase was writ in Shropshire stone,
Since Druid chaunts desponded in this glade
Or Tuscan general called that field his own,
 How long ago? How long?
How long since wanderers in the Stretton Hills
Met men of shaggy hair and savage jaw,
 With flint and copper prong,
Aiming behind their dikes and thorny grilles?
 Ah! those were days before the axe and saw,
 Then were the nights when this mid-forest town
 Held breath to hear the wolves come yelping down,
 And ponderous bears 'long Severn lifted paw,
 And nuzzling boars ran grunting through the shaw.

Ah me! full fifteen hundred times the wheat
Hath risen, and bowed, and fallen to human hunger
Since those imperial days were made complete.

The weary moon hath waxen old and younger
	These eighteen thousand times
Without a shrine to greet her gentle ray.
And other temples rose; to Power and Pelf,
	And chimed centurial chimes
Until their very bells are worn away.
While King by King lay cold on vaulted shelf
And wars closed wars, and many a Marmion fell,
And dearths and plagues holp sire and son to hell;
And old age stiffened many a lively elf
And many a poet's heart outdrained itself.

I had forgot that so remote an age
Beyond the horizon of our little sight,
Is far from us by no more spanless gauge
Than day and night, succeeding day and night,
	Until I looked on Thee,
Thou ghost of a dead city, or its husk!
But even as we could walk by field and hedge
	Hence to the distant sea
So, by the rote of common dawn and dusk,
We travel back to history's utmost edge.
Yea, when through thy old streets I took my way,
And recked a thousand years as yesterday,
Methought sage fancy wrought a sacrilege
To steal for me such godly privilege!

For here lie remnants from a banquet table –
Oysters and marrow-bones, and seeds of grape –
The statement of whose age must sound a fable;
And Samian jars, whose sheen and flawless shape
	Look fresh from potter's mould.
Plasters with Roman finger-marks impressed;
Bracelets, that from the warm Italian arm
	Might seem to be scarce cold;
And spears – the same that pushed the Cymry west –
Unblunted yet; with tools of forge and farm
Abandoned, as a man in sudden fear
Drops what he holds to help his swift career:

For sudden was Rome's flight, and wild the alarm.
The Saxon shock was like Vesuvius' qualm.

O ye who prate of modern art and craft
Mark well that Gaulish brooch, and test that screw!
Art's fairest buds on antique stem are graft.
Under the sun is nothing wholly new!
    At Viricon today
The village anvil rests on Roman base
And in a garden, may be seen a bower
    With pillars for its stay
That anciently in basilic had place.
The church's font is but a pagan dower:
A Temple's column, hollowed into this.
So is the glory of our artifice,
Our pleasure and our worship, but the flower
Of Roman custom and of Roman power.

O ye who laugh and, living as if Time
Meant but the twelve hours ticking round your dial,
Find it too short for thee, watch the sublime,
Slow, epochal time-registers awhile,
    Which are Antiquities.
O ye who weep and call all your life too long
And moan: Was ever sorrow like to mine?
    Muse on the memories
That sad sepulchral stones and ruins prolong.
Here might men drink of wonder like strong wine
And feel ephemeral troubles soothed and curbed.
Yet farmers, wroth to have their laws disturbed,
Are sooner roused for little loss to pine
Than we are moved by mighty woes long syne.

Above this reverend ground, what traveller checks?
Yet cities such as these one time would breed
Apocalyptic visions of world-wrecks.
Let Saxon men return to them, and heed!
    They slew and burnt,
But after, prized what Rome had given away

Out of her strength and her prosperity.
Have they yet learnt
The precious truth distilled from Rome's decay?
Ruins! On England's heart press heavily!
For Rome hath left us more than walls and words
And better yet shall leave; and more than herds
Or land or gold gave the Celts to us in fee;
E'en Blood, which makes poets sing and prophets see.

Inspection

'You! What d'you mean by this?' I rapped.
'You dare come on parade like this?'
'Please, sir, it's –' ''Old yer mouth,' the sergeant snapped.
'I takes 'is name, sir?' – 'Please, and then dismiss.'

Some days 'confined to camp' he got,
For being 'dirty on parade'.
He told me, afterwards, the damnèd spot
Was blood, his own. 'Well, blood is dirt,' I said.

'Blood's dirt,' he laughed, looking away,
Far off to where his wound had bled
And almost merged for ever into clay.
'The world is washing out its stains,' he said.
'It doesn't like our cheeks so red:
Young blood's its great objection.
But when we're duly white-washed, being dead,
The race will bear Field Marshal God's inspection.'

With an Identity Disc

If ever I had dreamed of my dead name
High in the heart of London, unsurpassed
By Time for ever, and the Fugitive, Fame,
There taking a long sanctuary at last,

I better that; and recollect with shame
How once I longed to hide it from life's heats
Under those holy cypresses, the same
That keep in shade the quiet place of Keats.

Now, rather, thank I God there is no risk
Of gravers scoring it with florid screed,
But let my death be memoried on this disc.
Wear it, sweet friend. Inscribe no date nor deed.
But let thy heart-beat kiss it night and day,
Until the name grow vague and wear away.

Anthem for Doomed Youth

What passing-bells for these who die as cattle?
– Only the monstrous anger of the guns.
Only the stuttering rifles' rapid rattle
Can patter out their hasty orisons.
No mockeries now for them; no prayers nor bells;
Nor any voice of mourning save the choirs, –
The shrill, demented choirs of wailing shells;
And bugles calling for them from sad shires.

What candles may be held to speed them all?
Not in the hands of boys but in their eyes
Shall shine the holy glimmers of goodbyes.
The pallor of girls' brows shall be their pall;
Their flowers the tenderness of patient minds,
And each slow dusk a drawing-down of blinds.

1914

War broke: and now the Winter of the world
With perishing great darkness closes in.
The foul tornado, centred at Berlin,
Is over all the width of Europe whirled,

Rending the sails of progress. Rent or furled
Are all Art's ensigns. Verse wails. Now begin
Famines of thought and feeling. Love's wine's thin.
The grain of human Autumn rots, down-hurled.

For after Spring had bloomed in early Greece,
And Summer blazed her glory out with Rome,
An Autumn softly fell, a harvest home,
A slow grand age, and rich with all increase.
But now, for us, wild Winter, and the need
Of sowings for new Spring, and blood for seed.

From My Diary, July 1914

Leaves
  Murmuring by myriads in the shimmering trees.
Lives
  Wakening with wonder in the Pyrenees.
Birds
  Cheerily chirping in the early day.
Bards
  Singing of summer, scything through the hay.
Bees
  Shaking the heavy dews from bloom and frond.
Boys
  Bursting the surface of the ebony pond.
Flashes
  Of swimmers carving through the sparkling cold.
Fleshes
  Gleaming with wetness to the morning gold.
A mead
  Bordered about with warbling waterbrooks.
A maid
  Laughing the love-laugh with me; proud of looks.
The heat
  Throbbing between the upland and the peak.

Her heart
    Quivering with passion to my pressèd cheek.
Braiding
    Of floating flames across the mountain brow.
Brooding
    Of stillness; and a sighing of the bough.
Stirs
    Of leaflets in the gloom; soft petal-showers;
Stars
    Expanding with the starr'd nocturnal flowers.

Apologia pro Poemate Meo

I, too, saw God through mud, –
    The mud that cracked on cheeks when wretches smiled.
    War brought more glory to their eyes than blood,
    And gave their laughs more glee than shakes a child.

Merry it was to laugh there –
    Where death becomes absurd and life absurder.
    For power was on us as we slashed bones bare
    Not to feel sickness or remorse of murder.

I, too, have dropped off Fear –
    Behind the barrage, dead as my platoon,
    And sailed my spirit surging light and clear
    Past the entanglement where hopes lay strewn;

And witnessed exultation –
    Faces that used to curse me, scowl for scowl,
    Shine and lift up with passion of oblation,
    Seraphic for an hour; though they were foul.

I have made fellowships –
  Untold of happy lovers in old song.
  For love is not the binding of fair lips
  With the soft silk of eyes that look and long,

By Joy, whose ribbon slips, –
  But wound with war's hard wire whose stakes are strong;
  Bound with the bandage of the arm that drips;
  Knit in the webbing of the rifle-thong.

I have perceived much beauty
  In the hoarse oaths that kept our courage straight;
  Heard music in the silentness of duty;
  Found peace where shell-storms spouted reddest spate.

Nevertheless, except you share
  With them in hell the sorrowful dark of hell,
  Whose world is but the trembling of a flare
  And heaven but as the highway for a shell,

You shall not hear their mirth:
  You shall not come to think them well content
  By any jest of mine. These men are worth
  Your tears. You are not worth their merriment.

Le Christianisme

So the church Christ was hit and buried
  Under its rubbish and its rubble.
In cellars, packed-up saints lie serried,
  Well out of hearing of our trouble.

One Virgin still immaculate
  Smiles on for war to flatter her.
She's halo'd with an old tin hat,
  But a piece of hell will batter her.

'Cramped in that funnelled hole'

Cramped in that funnelled hole, they watched the
dawn
Open jagged rim around; a yawn
Of death's jaws, which had all but swallowed them
Stuck in the bottom of his throat of phlegm.

They were in one of many mouths of Hell
Not seen of seem in visions; only felt
As teeth of traps; when bones and the dead are smelt
Under the mud where long ago they fell
Mixed with the sour sharp odour of the shell.

Hospital Barge

Budging the sluggard ripples of the Somme,
A barge round old Cérisy slowly slewed.
Softly her engines down the current screwed,
And chuckled softly with contented hum,
Till fairy tinklings struck their croonings dumb.
The waters rumpling at the stern subdued;
The lock-gate took her bulging amplitude;
Gently from out the gurgling lock she swum.

One reading by that calm bank shaded eyes
To watch her lessening westward quietly.
Then, as she neared the bend, her funnel screamed.
And that long lamentation made him wise
How unto Avalon, in agony,
Kings passed in the dark barge which Merlin
dreamed.

At a Calvary near the Ancre

One ever hangs where shelled roads part.
In this war He too lost a limb,
But His disciples hide apart;
And now the Soldiers bear with Him.

Near Golgotha strolls many a priest,
And in their faces there is pride
That they were flesh-marked by the Beast
By whom the gentle Christ's denied.

The scribes on all the people shove
And bawl allegiance to the state,
But they who love the greater love
Lay down their life; they do not hate.

Miners

There was a whispering in my hearth,
A sigh of the coal,
Grown wistful of a former earth
It might recall.

I listened for a tale of leaves
And smothered ferns,
Frond-forests, and the low sly lives
Before the fauns.

My fire might show steam-phantoms simmer
From Time's old cauldron,
Before the birds made nests in summer,
Or men had children.

But the coals were murmuring of their mine,
And moans down there
Of boys that slept wry sleep, and men
Writhing for air.

And I saw white bones in the cinder-shard,
Bones without number.
Many the muscled bodies charred,
And few remember.

I thought of all that worked dark pits
Of war, and died
Digging the rock where Death reputes
Peace lies indeed.

Comforted years will sit soft-chaired,
In rooms of amber;
The years will stretch their hands, well-cheered
By our life's ember;

The centuries will burn rich loads
With which we groaned,
Whose warmth shall lull their dreaming lids,
While songs are crooned;
But they will not dream of us poor lads,
Left in the ground.

The Letter

With B.E.F. June 10. Dear Wife,
(Oh blast this pencil. 'Ere, Bill, lend's a knife.)
I'm in the pink at present, dear.
I think the war will end this year.
We don't see much of them square-'eaded 'Uns.
We're out of harm's way, not bad fed.
I'm longing for a taste of your old buns.

(Say, Jimmie, spare's a bite of bread.)
There don't seem much to say just now.
(Yer what? Then don't, yer ruddy cow!
And give us back me cigarette!)
I'll soon be 'ome. You mustn't fret.
My feet's improvin', as I told you of.
We're out in rest now. Never fear.
(VRACH! By crumbs, but that was near.)
Mother might spare you half a sov.
Kiss Neil and Bert. When me and you –
(Eh? What the 'ell! Stand to? Stand to!
Jim, give's a hand with pack on, lad.
Guh! Christ! I'm hit. Take 'old. Aye, bad.
No, damn your iodine. Jim? 'Ere!
Write my old girl, Jim, there's a dear.)

Conscious

His fingers wake, and flutter; up the bed.
His eyes come open with a pull of will,
Helped by the yellow mayflowers by his head.
The blind-cord drawls across the window-sill . . .
What a smooth floor the ward has! What a rug!
Who is that talking somewhere out of sight?
Three flies are creeping round the shiny jug . . .
'Nurse! Doctor!' – 'Yes, all right, all right.'

But sudden evening blurs and fogs the air.
There seems no time to want a drink of water.
Nurse looks so far away. And here and there
Music and roses burst through crimson slaughter.
He can't remember where he saw blue sky . . .
The trench is narrower. Cold, he's cold; yet hot –
And there's no light to see the voices by . . .
There is no time to ask . . . he knows not what.

Dulce et Decorum Est

Bent double, like old beggars under sacks,
Knock-kneed, coughing like hags, we cursed through
sludge,
Till on the haunting flares we turned our backs
And towards our distant rest began to trudge.
Men marched asleep. Many had lost their boots
But limped on, blood-shod. All went lame; all blind;
Drunk with fatigue; deaf even to the hoots
Of tired, outstripped Five-nines that dropped behind.

Gas! GAS! Quick, boys! – An ecstasy of fumbling,
Fitting the clumsy helmets just in time;
But someone still was yelling out and stumbling,
And flound'ring like a man in fire or lime . . .
Dim, through the misty panes and thick green light,
As under a green sea, I saw him drowning.

In all my dreams, before my helpless sight,
He plunges at me, guttering, choking, drowning.

If in some smothering dreams you too could pace
Behind the wagon that we flung him in,
And watch the white eyes writhing in his face,
His hanging face, like a devil's sick of sin;
If you could hear, at every jolt, the blood
Come gargling from the froth-corrupted lungs,
Obscene as cancer, bitter as the cud
Of vile, incurable sores on innocent tongues, –
My friend, you would not tell with such high zest
To children ardent for some desperate glory,
The old Lie: Dulce et decorum est
Pro patria mori.

Insensibility

1

Happy are men who yet before they are killed
Can let their veins run cold.
Whom no compassion fleers
Or makes their feet
Sore on the alleys cobbled with their brothers.
The front line withers.
But they are troops who fade, not flowers,
For poets' tearful fooling:
Men, gaps for filling:
Losses, who might have fought
Longer; but no one bothers.

2

And some cease feeling
Even themselves or for themselves.
Dullness best solves
The tease and doubt of shelling,
And Chance's strange arithmetic
Comes simpler than the reckoning of their shilling.
They keep no check on armies' decimation.

3

Happy are these who lose imagination:
They have enough to carry with ammunition.
Their spirit drags no pack.
Their old wounds, save with cold, can not more ache.
Having seen all things red,
Their eyes are rid
Of the hurt of the colour of blood for ever.
And terror's first constriction over,

Their hearts remain small-drawn.
Their senses in some scorching cautery of battle
Now long since ironed,
Can laugh among the dying, unconcerned.

4

Happy the soldier home, with not a notion
How somewhere, every dawn, some men attack,
And many sighs are drained.
Happy the lad whose mind was never trained:
His days are worth forgetting more than not.
He sings along the march
Which we march taciturn, because of dusk,
The long, forlorn, relentless trend
From larger day to huger night.

5

We wise, who with a thought besmirch
Blood over all our soul,
How should we see our task
But through his blunt and lashless eyes?
Alive, he is not vital overmuch;
Dying, not mortal overmuch;
Nor sad, nor proud,
Nor curious at all.
He cannot tell
Old men's placidity from his.

6

But cursed are dullards whom no cannon stuns,
That they should be as stones.
Wretched are they, and mean
With paucity that never was simplicity.
By choice they made themselves immune
To pity and whatever moans in man

Before the last sea and the hapless stars;
Whatever mourns when many leave these shores;
Whatever shares
The eternal reciprocity of tears.

Strange Meeting

It seemed that out of battle I escaped
Down some profound dull tunnel, long since scooped
Through granites which titanic wars had groined.

Yet also there encumbered sleepers groaned,
Too fast in thought or death to be bestirred.
Then, as I probed them, one sprang up, and stared
With piteous recognition in fixed eyes,
Lifting distressful hands, as if to bless.
And by his smile, I knew that sullen hall, –
By his dead smile I knew we stood in Hell.

With a thousand pains that vision's face was grained;
Yet no blood reached there from the upper ground,
And no guns thumped, or down the flues made moan.
'Strange friend,' I said, 'here is no cause to mourn.'
'None,' said that other, 'save the undone years,
The hopelessness. Whatever hope is yours,
Was my life also; I went hunting wild
After the wildest beauty in the world,
Which lies not calm in eyes, or braided hair,
But mocks the steady running of the hour,
And if it grieves, grieves richlier than here.
For by my glee might many men have laughed,
And of my weeping something had been left,
Which must die now. I mean the truth untold,
The pity of war, the pity war distilled.
Now men will go content with what we spoiled,
Or, discontent, boil bloody, and be spilled.
They will be swift with swiftness of the tigress.

None will break ranks, though nations trek from progress.
Courage was mine, and I had mystery,
Wisdom was mine, and I had mastery:
To miss the march of this retreating world
Into vain citadels that are not walled.
Then, when much blood had clogged their chariot-wheels,
I would go up and wash them from sweet wells,
Even with truths that lie too deep for taint.
I would have poured my spirit without stint
But not through wounds; not on the cess of war.
Foreheads of men have bled where no wounds were.

'I am the enemy you killed, my friend.
I knew you in this dark: for so you frowned
Yesterday through me as you jabbed and killed.
I parried; but my hands were loath and cold.
Let us sleep now. . . .'

Asleep

Under his helmet, up against his pack,
After so many days of work and waking,
Sleep took him by the brow and laid him back.

There, in the happy no-time of his sleeping,
Death took him by the heart. There heaved a quaking
Of the aborted life within him leaping,
Then chest and sleepy arms once more fell slack.

And soon the slow, stray blood came creeping
From the intruding lead, like ants on track.

Whether his deeper sleep lie shaded by the shaking
Of great wings, and the thoughts that hung the stars,
High-pillowed on calm pillows of God's making,
Above these clouds, these rains, these sleets of lead,
And these winds' scimitars,

– Or whether yet his thin and sodden head
Confuses more and more with the low mould,
His hair being one with the grey grass
Of finished fields, and wire-scrags rusty-old,
Who knows? Who hopes? Who troubles? Let it pass!
He sleeps. He sleeps less tremulous, less cold,
Than we who wake, and waking say Alas!

Arms and the Boy

Let the boy try along this bayonet-blade
How cold steel is, and keen with hunger of blood;
Blue with all malice, like a madman's flash;
And thinly drawn with famishing for flesh.

Lend him to stroke these blind, blunt bullet-leads,
Which long to nuzzle in the hearts of lads,
Or give him cartridges whose fine zinc teeth
Are sharp with sharpness of grief and death.

For his teeth seem for laughing round an apple.
There lurk no claws behind his fingers supple;
And God will grow no talons at his heels,
Nor antlers through the thickness of his curls.

The Show

We have fallen in the dreams the ever-living
Breathe on the tarnished mirror of the world,
And then smooth out with ivory hands and sigh.

W. B. YEATS

My soul looked down from a vague height, with Death,
As unremembering how I rose or why,
And saw a sad land, weak with sweats of dearth,
Grey, cratered like the moon with hollow woe,
And pitted with great pocks and scabs of plagues.

Across its beard, that horror of harsh wire,
There moved thin caterpillars, slowly uncoiled.
It seemed they pushed themselves to be as plugs
Of ditches, where they writhed and shrivelled, killed.

By them had slimy paths been trailed and scraped
Round myriad warts that might be little hills.

From gloom's last dregs these long-strung creatures crept,
And vanished out of dawn down hidden holes.

(And smell came up from those foul openings
As out of mouths, or deep wounds deepening.)

On dithering feet upgathered, more and more,
Brown strings, towards strings of grey, with bristling spines,
All migrants from green fields, intent on mire.

Those that were grey, of more abundant spawns,
Ramped on the rest and ate them and were eaten.

I saw their bitten backs curve, loop, and straighten.
I watched those agonies curl, lift and flatten.

Whereat, in terror what that sight might mean,
I reeled and shivered earthward like a feather.

And Death fell with me, like a deepening moan.
And He, picking a manner of worm, which half had hid
Its bruises in the earth, but crawled no further,
Showed me its feet, the feet of many men,
And the fresh-severed head of it, my head.

Futility

Move him into the sun –
Gently its touch awoke him once,
At home, whispering of fields half-sown.
Always it woke him, even in France,
Until this morning and this snow.
If anything might rouse him now
The kind old sun will know.

Think how it wakes the seeds –
Woke once the clays of a cold star.
Are limbs, so dear achieved, are sides
Full-nerved, still warm, too hard to stir?
Was it for this the clay grew tall?
– O what made fatuous sunbeams toil
To break earth's sleep at all?

The End

After the blast of lightning from the east,
The flourish of loud clouds, the Chariot Throne;
After the drums of time have rolled and ceased,
And by the bronze west long retreat is blown,
Shall Life renew these bodies? Of a truth,
All death will he annul, all tears assuage?
Or fill these void veins full again with youth,
And wash, with an immortal water, age?

When I do ask white Age, he saith not so:
'My head hangs weighed with snow.'
And when I hearken to the Earth, she saith:
'My fiery heart shrinks, aching. It is death.
Mine ancient scars shall not be glorified,
Nor my titanic tears, the seas, be dried.'

S.I.W.

I will to the King,
And offer him consolation in his trouble,
For that man there has set his teeth to die,
And being one that hates obedience,
Discipline, and orderliness of life,
I cannot mourn him.

W. B. YEATS

I. The Prologue

Patting goodbye, doubtless they told the lad
He'd always show the Hun a brave man's face;
Father would sooner him dead than in disgrace, –
Was proud to see him going, aye, and glad.
Perhaps his mother whimpered how she'd fret
Until he got a nice safe wound to nurse.
Sisters would wish girls too could shoot, charge, curse . . .
Brothers – would send his favourite cigarette.
Each week, month after month, they wrote the same,
Thinking him sheltered in some Y.M. Hut,
Because he said so, writing on his butt
Where once an hour a bullet missed its aim.
And misses teased the hunger of his brain.
His eyes grew old with wincing, and his hand
Reckless with ague. Courage leaked, as sand
From the best sandbags after years of rain.
But never leave, wound, fever, trench-foot, shock,
Untrapped the wretch. And death seemed still withheld
For torture of lying machinally shelled,
At the pleasure of this world's Powers who'd
run amok.

He'd seen men shoot their hands, on night patrol.
Their people never knew. Yet they were vile.
'Death sooner than dishonour, that's the style!'
So Father said.

II. The Action

One dawn, our wire patrol
Carried him. This time, Death had not missed.
We could do nothing but wipe his bleeding cough.
Could it be accident? – Rifles go off . . .
Not sniped? No. (Later they found the English ball.)

III. The Poem

It was the reasoned crisis of his soul
Against more days of inescapable thrall,
Against infrangibly wired and blind trench wall
Curtained with fire, roofed in with creeping fire,
Slow grazing fire, that would not burn him whole
But kept him for death's promises and scoff,
And life's half-promising, and both their riling.

IV. The Epilogue

With him they buried the muzzle his teeth had kissed,
And truthfully wrote the mother, 'Tim died smiling.'

The Next War

War's a joke for me and you,
While we know such dreams are true.
SIEGFRIED SASSOON

Out there, we walked quite friendly up to Death, –
Sat down and ate beside him, cool and bland, –
Pardoned his spilling mess-tins in our hand.
We've sniffed the green thick odour of his breath, –

Our eyes wept, but our courage didn't writhe.
He's spat at us with bullets, and he's coughed
Shrapnel. We chorused if he sang aloft,
We whistled while he shaved us with his scythe.

Oh, Death was never enemy of ours!
We laughed at him, we leagued with him, old chum.
No soldier's paid to kick against His powers.
We laughed, – knowing that better men would come,
And greater wars: when every fighter brags
He fights on Death, for lives; not men, for flags.

Greater Love

Red lips are not so red
As the stained stones kissed by the English dead.
Kindness of wooed and wooer
Seems shame to their love pure.
O Love, your eyes lose lure
When I behold eyes blinded in my stead!

Your slender attitude
Trembles not exquisite like limbs knife-skewed,
Rolling and rolling there
Where God seems not to care;
Till the fierce love they bear
Cramps them in death's extreme decrepitude.

Your voice sings not so soft, –
Though even as wind murmuring through raftered loft, –
Your dear voice is not dear,
Gentle, and evening clear,
As theirs whom none now hear,
Now earth has stopped their piteous mouths that coughed.

Heart, you were never hot
    Nor large, nor full like hearts made great with shot;
And though your hand be pale,
Paler are all which trail
Your cross through flame and hail:
    Weep, you may weep, for you may touch them not.

The Last Laugh

'Oh! Jesus Christ! I'm hit,' he said; and died.
Whether he vainly cursed or prayed indeed,
    The Bullets chirped – In vain, vain, vain!
    Machine-guns chuckled – Tut-tut! Tut-tut!
    And the Big Gun guffawed.

Another sighed – 'O Mother, – Mother, – Dad!'
Then smiled at nothing, childlike, being dead.
    And the lofty Shrapnel-cloud
    Leisurely gestured, – Fool!
    And the splinters spat, and tittered.

'My Love!' One moaned. Love-languid seemed his mood,
Till slowly lowered, his whole face kissed the mud.
    And the Bayonet's long teeth grinned;
    Rabbles of Shells hooted and groaned;
    And the Gas hissed.

Mental Cases

Who are these? Why sit they here in twilight?
Wherefore rock they, purgatorial shadows,
Drooping tongues from jaws that slob their relish,
Baring teeth that leer like skulls' teeth wicked?
Stroke on stroke of pain, – but what slow panic,

Gouged these chasms round their fretted sockets?
Ever from their hair and through their hands' palms
Misery swelters. Surely we have perished
Sleeping, and walk hell; but who these hellish?

– These are men whose minds the Dead have ravished.
Memory fingers in their hair of murders,
Multitudinous murders they once witnessed.
Wading sloughs of flesh these helpless wander,
Treading blood from lungs that had loved laughter.
Always they must see these things and hear them,
Batter of guns and shatter of flying muscles,
Carnage incomparable, and human squander
Rucked too thick for these men's extrication.

Therefore still their eyeballs shrink tormented
Back into their brains, because on their sense
Sunlight seems a blood-smear; night comes blood-black;
Dawn breaks open like a wound that bleeds afresh.
– Thus their heads wear this hilarious, hideous,
Awful falseness of set-smiling corpses.
– Thus their hands are plucking at each other;
Picking at the rope-knouts of their scourging;
Snatching after us who smote them, brother,
Pawing us who dealt them war and madness.

The Chances

I 'mind as how the night before that show
Us five got talkin'; we was in the know.
'Ah well,' says Jimmy, and he's seen some scrappin',
'There ain't no more than five things as can happen, –
You get knocked out; else wounded, bad or cushy;
Scuppered; or nowt except you're feelin' mushy.'

One of us got the knock-out, blown to chops;
One lad was hurt, like, losin' both his props;
And one – to use the word of hypocrites –
Had the misfortune to be took by Fritz.
Now me, I wasn't scratched, praise God Almighty,
Though next time please I'll thank Him for a blighty.
But poor old Jim, he's livin' and he's not;
He reckoned he'd five chances, and he had:
He's wounded, killed, and pris'ner, all the lot,
The flamin' lot all rolled in one. Jim's mad.

The Send-Off

Down the close darkening lanes they sang their way
To the siding-shed,
And lined the train with faces grimly gay.

Their breasts were stuck all white with wreath and spray
As men's are, dead.

Dull porters watched them, and a casual tramp
Stood staring hard,
Sorry to miss them from the upland camp.

Then, unmoved, signals nodded, and a lamp
Winked to the guard.

So secretly, like wrongs hushed-up, they went.
They were not ours:
We never heard to which front these were sent;

Nor there if they yet mock what women meant
Who gave them flowers.

Shall they return to beating of great bells
In wild train-loads?
A few, a few, too few for drums and yells,

May creep back, silent, to village wells,
Up half-known roads.

The Parable of the Old Man and the Young

So Abram rose, and clave the wood, and went,
And took the fire with him, and a knife.
And as they sojourned both of them together,
Isaac the first-born spake and said, My Father,
Behold the preparations, fire and iron,
But where the lamb, for this burnt-offering?
Then Abram bound the youth with belts and straps,
And builded parapets and trenches there,
And stretchèd forth the knife to slay his son.
When lo! an Angel called him out of heaven,
Saying, Lay not thy hand upon the lad,
Neither do anything to him, thy son.
Behold! Caught in a thicket by its horns,
A Ram. Offer the Ram of Pride instead.

But the old man would not so, but slew his son,
And half the seed of Europe, one by one.

Disabled

He sat in a wheeled chair, waiting for dark,
And shivered in his ghastly suit of grey,
Legless, sewn short at elbow. Through the park
Voices of boys rang saddening like a hymn,
Voices of play and pleasure after day,
Till gathering sleep had mothered them from him.

* * *

About this time Town used to swing so gay
When glow-lamps budded in the light blue trees,
And girls glanced lovelier as the air grew dim, –
In the old times, before he threw away his knees.
Now he will never feel again how slim
Girls' waists are, or how warm their subtle hands.
All of them touch him like some queer disease.

* * *

There was an artist silly for his face,
For it was younger than his youth, last year.
Now, he is old; his back will never brace;
He's lost his colour very far from here,
Poured it down shell-holes till the veins ran dry,
And half his lifetime lapsed in the hot race
And leap of purple spurted from his thigh.

* * *

One time he liked a blood-smear down his leg,
After the matches, carried shoulder-high.
It was after football, when he'd drunk a peg,
He thought he'd better join. – He wonders why.
Someone had said he'd look a god in kilts,

That's why; and maybe, too, to please his Meg,
Aye, that was it, to please the giddy jilts
He asked to join. He didn't have to beg;
Smiling they wrote his lie: aged nineteen years.
Germans he scarcely thought of; all their guilt,
And Austria's, did not move him. And no fears
Of Fear came yet. He thought of jewelled hilts
For daggers in plaid socks; of smart salutes;
And care of arms; and leave; and pay arrears;
Esprit de corps; and hints for young recruits.
And soon, he was drafted out with drums and cheers.

* * *

Some cheered him home, but not as crowds cheer Goal.
Only a solemn man who brought him fruits
Thanked him; and then enquired about his soul.

* * *

Now, he will spend a few sick years in institutes,
And do what things the rules consider wise,
And take whatever pity they may dole.
Tonight he noticed how the women's eyes
Passed from him to the strong men that were whole.
How cold and late it is! Why don't they come
And put him into bed? Why don't they come?

A Terre
(being the philosophy of many soldiers)

Sit on the bed. I'm blind, and three parts shell.
Be careful; can't shake hands now; never shall.
Both arms have mutinied against me, – brutes.
My fingers fidget like ten idle brats.

I tried to peg out soldierly, – no use!
One dies of war like any old disease.
This bandage feels like pennies on my eyes.
I have my medals? – Discs to make eyes close.
My glorious ribbons? – Ripped from my own back
In scarlet shreds. (That's for your poetry book.)

A short life and a merry one, my buck!
We used to say we'd hate to live dead-old, –
Yet now . . . I'd willingly be puffy, bald,
And patriotic. Buffers catch from boys
At least the jokes hurled at them. I suppose
Little I'd ever teach a son, but hitting,
Shooting, war, hunting, all the arts of hurting.
Well, that's what I learnt, – that, and making money.

Your fifty years ahead seem none too many?
Tell me how long I've got? God! For one year
To help myself to nothing more than air!
One Spring! Is one too good to spare, too long?
Spring wind would work its own way to my lung,
And grow me legs as quick as lilac-shoots.

My servant's lamed, but listen how he shouts!
When I'm lugged out, he'll still be good for that.
Here in this mummy-case, you know, I've thought
How well I might have swept his floors for ever.
I'd ask no nights off when the bustle's over,
Enjoying so the dirt. Who's prejudiced
Against a grimed hand when his own's quite dust,
Less live than specks that in the sun-shafts turn,
Less warm than dust that mixes with arms' tan?
I'd love to be a sweep, now, black as Town,
Yes, or a muckman. Must I be his load?

O Life, Life, let me breathe, – a dug-out rat!
Not worse than ours the lives rats lead –
Nosing along at night down some safe rut,
They find a shell-proof home before they rot.
Dead men may envy living mites in cheese,
Or good germs even. Microbes have their joys,
And subdivide, and never come to death.
Certainly flowers have the easiest time on earth.
'I shall be one with nature, herb, and stone,'
Shelley would tell me. Shelley would be stunned:
The dullest Tommy hugs that fancy now.
'Pushing up daisies' is their creed, you know.

To grain, then, go my fat, to buds my sap,
For all the usefulness there is in soap.
D'you think the Boche will ever stew man-soup?
Some day, no doubt, if . . .
Friend, be very sure
I shall be better off with plants that share
More peaceably the meadow and the shower.
Soft rains will touch me, – as they could touch once,
And nothing but the sun shall make me ware.
Your guns may crash around me. I'll not hear;
Or, if I wince, I shall not know I wince.

Don't take my soul's poor comfort for your jest.
Soldiers may grow a soul when turned to fronds,
But here the thing's best left at home with friends.

My soul's a little grief, grappling your chest,
To climb your throat on sobs; easily chased
On other sighs and wiped by fresher winds.

Carry my crying spirit till it's weaned
To do without what blood remained these wounds.

The Kind Ghosts

She sleeps on soft, last breaths; but no ghost looms
Out of the stillness of her palace wall,
Her wall of boys on boys and dooms on dooms.

She dreams of golden gardens and sweet glooms,
Not marvelling why her roses never fall
Nor what red mouths were torn to make their blooms.

The shades keep down which well might roam her hall.
Quiet their blood lies in her crimson rooms
And she is not afraid of their footfall.

They move not from her tapestries, their pall,
Nor pace her terraces, their hecatombs,
Lest aught she be disturbed, or grieved at all.

Exposure

Our brains ache, in the merciless iced east winds that knive us . . .
Wearied we keep awake because the night is silent . . .
Low, drooping flares confuse our memory of the salient . . .
Worried by silence, sentries whisper, curious, nervous,
  But nothing happens.

Watching, we hear the mad gusts tugging on the wire,
Like twitching agonies of men among its brambles.
Northward, incessantly, the flickering gunnery rumbles,
Far off, like a dull rumour of some other war.
  What are we doing here?

The poignant misery of dawn begins to grow . . .
We only know war lasts, rain soaks, and clouds sag stormy.
Dawn massing in the east her melancholy army
Attacks once more in ranks on shivering ranks of grey,
  But nothing happens.

Sudden successive flights of bullets streak the silence.
Less deathly than the air that shudders black with snow,
With sidelong flowing flakes that flock, pause, and renew;
We watch them wandering up and down the wind's nonchalance,
But nothing happens.

Pale flakes with fingering stealth come feeling for our faces –
We cringe in holes, back on forgotten dreams, and stare, snow-dazed,
Deep into grassier ditches. So we drowse, sun-dozed,
Littered with blossoms trickling where the blackbird fusses,
– Is it that we are dying?

Slowly our ghosts drag home: glimpsing the sunk fires, glozed
With crusted dark-red jewels; crickets jingle there;
For hours the innocent mice rejoice: the house is theirs;
Shutters and doors, all closed: on us the doors are closed, –
We turn back to our dying.

Since we believe not otherwise can kind fires burn;
Nor ever suns smile true on child, or field, or fruit.
For God's invincible spring our love is made afraid;
Therefore, not loath we lie out here; therefore were born,
For love of God seems dying.

Tonight, this frost will fasten on this mud and us,
Shrivelling many hands, puckering foreheads crisp.
The burying-party, picks and shovels in shaking grasp,
Pause over half-known faces. All their eyes are ice,
But nothing happens.

The Sentry

We'd found an old Boche dug-out, and he knew,
And gave us hell; for shell on frantic shell
Lit full on top, but never quite burst through.

Rain, guttering down in waterfalls of slime,
Kept slush waist-high and rising hour by hour,
And choked the steps too thick with clay to climb.
What murk of air remained stank old, and sour
With fumes from whizz-bangs, and the smell of men
Who'd lived there years, and left their curse in the den,
If not their corpses . . .
There we herded from the blast
Of whizz-bangs; but one found our door at last, –
Buffeting eyes and breath, snuffing the candles,
And thud! flump! thud! down the steep steps came
thumping
And sploshing in the flood, deluging muck,
The sentry's body; then his rifle, handles
Of old Boche bombs, and mud in ruck on ruck.
We dredged it up, for dead, until he whined,
'O sir – my eyes, – I'm blind, – I'm blind, – I'm blind.'
Coaxing, I held a flame against his lids
And said if he could see the least blurred light
He was not blind; in time they'd get all right.
'I can't,' he sobbed. Eyeballs, huge-bulged like squids',
Watch my dreams still, – yet I forgot him there
In posting Next for duty, and sending a scout
To beg a stretcher somewhere, and flound'ring about
To other posts under the shrieking air.

Those other wretches, how they bled and spewed,
And one who would have drowned himself for good, –
I try not to remember these things now.
Let Dread hark back for one word only: how,
Half-listening to that sentry's moans and jumps,
And the wild chattering of his shivered teeth,
Renewed most horribly whenever crumps
Pummelled the roof and slogged the air beneath, –
Through the dense din, I say, we heard him shout
'I see your lights!' – But ours had long gone out.

Smile, Smile, Smile

Head to limp head, the sunk-eyed wounded scanned
Yesterday's *Mail;* the casualties (typed small)
And (large) Vast Booty from our Latest Haul.
Also, they read of Cheap Homes, not yet planned,
'For', said the paper, 'when this war is done
The men's first instincts will be making homes.
Meanwhile their foremost need is aerodromes,
It being certain war has but begun.
Peace would do wrong to our undying dead, –
The sons we offered might regret they died
If we got nothing lasting in their stead.
We must be solidly indemnified.
Though all be worthy Victory which all bought,
We rulers sitting in this ancient spot
Would wrong our very selves if we forgot
The greatest glory will be theirs who fought,
Who kept this nation in integrity.'
Nation? – The half-limbed readers did not chafe
But smiled at one another curiously
Like secret men who know their secret safe.
(This is the thing they know and never speak,
That England one by one had fled to France,
Not many elsewhere now, save under France.)
Pictures of these broad smiles appear each week,
And people in whose voice real feeling rings
Say: How they smile! They're happy now, poor things.

Spring Offensive

Halted against the shade of a last hill
They fed, and eased of pack-loads, were at ease;
And leaning on the nearest chest or knees
Carelessly slept.
But many there stood still

To face the stark blank sky beyond the ridge,
Knowing their feet had come to the end of the world.
Marvelling they stood, and watched the long grass swirled
By the May breeze, murmurous with wasp and midge;
And though the summer oozed into their veins
Like an injected drug for their bodies' pains,
Sharp on their souls hung the imminent ridge of grass,
Fearfully flashed the sky's mysterious glass.

Hour after hour they ponder the warm field
And the far valley behind, where buttercups
Had blessed with gold their slow boots coming up;
When even the little brambles would not yield
But clutched and clung to them like sorrowing arms.
They breathe like trees unstirred.

Till like a cold gust thrills the little word
At which each body and its soul begird
And tighten them for battle. No alarms
Of bugles, no high flags, no clamorous haste, –
Only a lift and flare of eyes that faced
The sun, like a friend with whom their love is done.
O larger shone that smile against the sun, –
Mightier than his whose bounty these have spurned.

So, soon they topped the hill, and raced together
Over an open stretch of herb and heather
Exposed. And instantly the whole sky burned
With fury against them; earth set sudden cups
In thousands for their blood; and the green slope
Chasmed and deepened sheer to infinite space.

Of them who running on that last high place
Breasted the surf of bullets, or went up
On the hot blast and fury of hell's upsurge,
Or plunged and fell away past this world's verge,
Some say God caught them even before they fell.

But what say such as from existence' brink
Ventured but drave too swift to sink,
The few who rushed in the body to enter hell,
And there out-fiending all its fiends and flames
With superhuman inhumanities,
Long-famous glories, immemorial shames –
And crawling slowly back, have by degrees
Regained cool peaceful air in wonder –
Why speak not they of comrades that went under?

Preface

This book is not about heroes. English poetry is not yet fit to speak of them.

Nor is it about deeds, or lands, nor anything about glory, honour, might, majesty, dominion, or power, except War.

Above all I am not concerned with Poetry.

My subject is War, and the pity of War.

The Poetry is in the pity.

Yet these elegies are to this generation in no sense consolatory. They may be to the next. All a poet can do today is warn. That is why the true Poets must be truthful.

(If I thought the letter of this book would last, I might have used proper names; but if the spirit of it survives – survives Prussia – my ambition and those names will have achieved fresher fields than Flanders. . . .)

Notes

IVOR GURNEY

Note on the Texts

Ivor Gurney published two volumes of poetry in his lifetime: *Severn & Somme* (Sidgwick & Jackson, 1917) and *War's Embers* (Sidgwick & Jackson, 1919). Numerous individual poems were published in periodicals such as the *Royal College of Music Magazine*, the *London Mercury*, *Music and Letters* and the *Spectator*.

The cataloguing and ordering of Gurney's work has been complex because of the various hands that have been involved in preserving it and his reputation, both poetic and musical. Versions of poems exist variously in manuscript and typescript, some of which include his handwritten amendments and additions, and others now only in a printed version. He was known for endlessly revisiting and revising his poems, causing difficulty for editors both in his lifetime and posthumously.

Gurney's two published volumes were compilations of poems he sent to Marion Scott while on active service. As P. J. Kavanagh argues: 'Scott plays a central part in the history of Gurney and his work. It was she who kept and transcribed his music and poetry for the rest of his life. That we have any Gurney at all is largely owing to her.'[1] Their correspondence details their discussions about various aspects of the poems, Gurney usually deferring to the opinion of Scott, whom he presumably felt the more experienced editorial voice. Of the war poems, he told her: 'I *never* keep a copy of these things. I get them off my chest, and send them to you.'[2] The Gurney Archive in Gloucester contain his copies of these two volumes, in which he has added his own notations, mainly citing at the end of each poem the place of its composition, but in some cases making more substantial revisions. The poems from *Severn & Somme* and *War's Embers* reprinted here are on the whole as they appeared in 1917 and 1919 respectively. In a few instances, indicated in the Notes, we have reinstated words or punctuation from Gurney's original manuscripts. The places of composition listed are taken from Gurney's annotations in his own copies of the two texts, though their accuracy cannot be verified.

After the War, he planned a third volume, comprised of poems composed between 1919 and 1922. These were submitted to Sidgwick & Jackson in 1922 but rejected. He shortened the volume, but this too was rejected by the publisher. Gurney tried to interest others in his poems, asking for help with publishers from Edward Marsh and Edmund Blunden, and others tried to publish collections, including Marion Scott, who in 1928 prepared a typescript for Gollancz, a project that never materialized. But even in his asylum years, from 1922 until his death, Gurney's poems appeared fairly regularly in print, particularly in the *London Mercury*, its editor J. C. Squire being 'the staunchest of [Gurney's] supporters in London'.[3] Squire also included his poems in the collections, *Selections of Modern Poets* (1921 and 1924) and *Younger Poets of Today* (1932).

During his asylum years, Gurney continued to write new poems and revise old ones. Marion Scott saw it as her mission to preserve as many of his manuscripts as possible. His musical work too was published and performed, mainly through the efforts of Scott and Gerald Finzi.[4] In 1938, shortly after his death, a special issue of *Music and Letters* was devoted to Gurney. The oft-told story of how he was too ill even to unwrap the parcel of proofs has been challenged by newly discovered evidence in the Gloucester Archives: the letter, which Marion Scott enclosed with the proofs, was used by Gurney to reply to Scott.

Philip Lancaster, who has catalogued all the material in the Gurney Archives, identifies three periods in Gurney's work: 1914–October 1918 (the War); November 1918–September 1922 (a new departure for his writing); September 1922–6 (the asylum poems). One poem from 1929 is extant, written on the back of a letter from Hubert Foss. From 1927, Gurney wrote a large number of essays, but a great deal of work (chamber music, symphonies, poems) from 1926 (and possibly later) was destroyed by Joy Finzi in about 1958 during her cataloguing of the poems after her husband's death, because it was 'incoherent and useless'. Gerald Finzi had believed that there were some parts of Gurney's writing 'that it would be better for them not to be published'.[5]

Subsequent editors of Gurney's work include Edmund Blunden, whose *Poems by Ivor Gurney* (London, 1954) brought together

78 poems, many of them previously unpublished, though some regarded Blunden's selection as 'eccentric'.[6] Leonard Clark's *Poems of Ivor Gurney* (London, 1973) included about half of Blunden's selection as well as his preface, but added 97 previously unpublished poems. The *Collected Poems of Ivor Gurney* was published by Oxford University Press in 1982. Chosen and edited by Kavanagh, who had access to material unavailable either to Blunden or Clark, the *Collected Poems* contains more than 300 poems, including those chosen by Blunden and Clark, with others selected from the archive. A revised and corrected paperback was published in 1984 and a fully revised version in 2004. Kavanagh also introduced a *Selected Poems* (London, 1990 and 1997).

In 1986, Mid Nag/Carcanet published *Severn & Somme* and *War's Embers*, edited by Thornton, together in one volume. Thornton and George Walter edited *'Best Poems' and 'The Book of Five Makings'* (Manchester, 1999), the contents of which were taken from two notebooks of 1925–6. *80 Poems or So* (Manchester, 1997), edited by Walter and Thornton, reconstructed a typescript of Gurney's 1922 unpublished 'third book'.

An Everyman edition, selected and edited by Walter, was published in 1996 and contained 146 poems, some previously unpublished. *Rewards of Wonder: Poems of Cotswold, France, London* (Manchester, 2000), again edited by Walter, was a reconstructed typescript of a collection made by Gurney in 1923–4, including many revised poems.

Severn & Somme and *War's Embers*, along with manuscripts and correspondence, have been scanned and are available for study online at the First World War Poetry Digital Archive (http://www.oucs.ox.ac.uk/ww1lit/). Tim Kendall and Philip Lancaster are editing Gurney's *Complete Poetry* for Oxford University Press. This three-volume edition will bring together all of Gurney's work for the first time in an authoritative edition. Gerald Finzi wrote that

> the sorting has been even more difficult than I expected, chiefly because there is comparatively little one can really be sure is bad. Even the late 1925 asylum songs, though they get more and more involved [. . .] have a curious coherence, which makes it difficult to know whether they are really over the border. I think the eventual 'difficulty' in editing the later Gurney may be great: a neat mind could smooth away the queerness [. . .] yet time and familiarity will show something not so mistaken after all, about the queer and odd things.[7]

NOTES

1. Kavanagh, p. xxii.
2. Thornton, *Ivor Gurney: Collected Letters*, p. 170.
3. George Walter and R. K. R. Thornton, *Ivor Gurney: 80 Poems or So* (Manchester, 1997), p. 15.
4. The relationship between Gurney's two champions, however, was not an easy one. Pamela Blevins's joint biography, Ivor Gurney and Marion Scott (2008), poignantly chronicles the difficulties and rescues Scott herself from being a footnote in music and literary history.
5. Kavanagh, p. xxxvii.
6. Ibid., p. xxxviii.
7. Ibid.

To the Poet before Battle

Written in July or early August 1915 at Chelmsford, this poem was included in Gurney's letter to Marion Scott of 3 August 1915. He asked: 'Please criticise this very frankly, and with no eye on Wordsworth's "September 1802" "London 1802" "It is not to be thought of", "October 1803" "November 1806", or any such. It is not meant to be complete' (Thornton, pp. 29–30). That Gurney's own eye was on these poems is shown by the archaic, Wordsworthian diction of his sonnet and, specifically, by two echoes.

1. *the hour*: Cf. Wordsworth, 'London, 1802' (line 1): 'Milton! Thou shouldst be living at this hour'.

4. *Unstirred . . . drums*: Reinstated original line, which Gurney allowed Scott to change to 'Unstirred by the rattle of the rolling drums', though he remarked, 'I do not understand the objection to it.'

14. *crown of honour*: Cf. also Wordsworth, 'November, 1806' (line 14): 'And honour which they do not understand'.

Strange Service

Probably written in July 1916 at Tilleloy, Gurney included this in his letter to Marion Scott of 27 July 1916 (Thornton, pp. 124–7). It, too, shows the general influence of Wordsworth's sonnets mentioned above. 'England' (line 1) is the 'Mother' (17), and the 'Cotswold Hills' (2) dominate an area of great natural beauty at the centre of Gurney's home county of Gloucestershire. Before *Severn & Somme* was chosen as the title for his first collection, 'Strange Service' was considered, and Scott continued to refer to the work-in-progress in this way. Gurney wrote to her: 'So you have decided to call the book "Strange Service", which is a very exact description of the feeling that made the book; it would sell better as "Severn & Somme" perhaps, but that is your business; you are my War Cabinet but far more subtle than the real' (Thornton, p. 288; Blevins, p. 100). Hawlin calls 'Strange Service' 'a beautiful and intense meditation on the poet's love of the "secret beauty" of Gloucestershire and the Severn, and through them, of England'. It is 'the one truly Whitmanesque poem' in the collection, prefiguring the later, more intense influence the American poet would have on Gurney (Hawlin, pp. 35–6); see 'To Long Island First' and 'Walt Whitman'.

1. *England, that you bore me*: A reference, perhaps, to Rupert Brooke's '1914' sonnet 'The Soldier' and its opening declaration:

> If I should die, think only this of me:
> That there's some corner of a foreign field
> That is for ever England. There shall be
> In that rich earth a richer dust concealed [. . .]

15. *In my deep heart*: Gurney may have had Yeats's line from 'The Lake of Innisfree' (1890) in mind: 'I hear it in the deep heart's core.'

Bach and the Sentry

Probably written early in November 1916, east of Laventie; a copy was included in the envelope of Gurney's letter of 8 November 1916 to Scott.

2. *that most dearest Prelude*: Possibly a reference to Wordsworth as well as any of several of Bach's compositions.
5. *music-making*: No doubt refers to composition as well as performance.

Song and Pain

Probably written in January 1917 at Crucifix Corner, the poem was included in Gurney's letter of 7 January 1917 to Scott. In his letter of 19 January to her, he wrote, 'It surprises me that you like "Song and Pain" best. It seems the least of those three.' He referred to the poem as 'Pain and Song' in two other letters to Scott regarding the arrangement of *Severn & Somme*, in which he suggested the poem 'may very well come out' (Thornton, p. 230), but it remained in the collection. Clark titled the poem 'Song of Pain'.

Song ['Only the wanderer']

Probably written in January 1917 at Caulaincourt and sent in Gurney's letter of 18 January 1917 to Scott. Set to music as 'Severn Meadows' in March 1917, it expresses 'a tender cry of longing for Gloucestershire's fields and meadows [. . .] Words and music in this song share equally in poignancy and absolute rightness' (Hurd, p. 78).

1. *the wanderer*: Many Georgian poets, including Gurney and Edward Thomas (see 'The Mangel-bury', line 1 and note), were inveterate walkers, traversing miles of countryside that inspired their writing.
8. O *Severn meadows*: See also 'Strange Service', line 2.

Ballad of the Three Spectres

Written in February 1917 at the Somme, this was sent in a letter to Scott of 15 February 1917. Gurney asked her on 23 February, 'Has "The Ballad of the Three Spectres" thrilled you as I wish? Is it Border-Ballady?' (Thornton, p. 218). Hurd argues that the 'ballad hits on a truth almost too terrible to contemplate – for in it, darkly, Ivor Gurney foresaw his own fate' (pp. 115–16).

1. *Ovillers*: A village in northern France that the 8th Division of the British Expeditionary Force attacked on 1 July 1916 during the Battle of the Somme. The casualty rate was very high and the village was not taken until 17 July.
8. *a Nice Blighty*: A non-fatal wound serious enough to secure a soldier's return to England. 'Blighty' is also the slang term for England itself. It was used sentimentally throughout the Great War to refer to home and featured in such songs as 'Take Me Back to Dear Old Blighty'. Coined during the British Raj in India, 'blighty' is derived from the Hindustani word *bilayati* meaning 'foreign land'.
12. *Picardie*: A variation of the spelling of Picardy, a region in northern France. Like 'Blighty' it had sentimental associations despite the violence that destroyed its landscape. Songs such as 'The Roses of Picardy' suggest a longing for a more innocent time.
20. *spake verity*: A prevision perhaps of Gurney's fifteen years in the asylum.

Time and the Soldier

Probably written in January 1917 at Crucifix Corner and included in a letter to Scott of 21 January 1917. The last three stanzas, with some alteration, were sent in a letter in February to Ethel Lilian Voynich, novelist and ameteur composer, who was a friend of Gurney's from the Royal College of Music: '"Time and the Soldier" I think will improve on you: it is W. H. Davies, but stronger; and one of my best' (Thornton, p. 202).

1–2 *How slow . . . faster*: W. H. Davies's poem 'Leisure' regrets that 'We have no time to stand and stare'.

After-Glow

Written in January 1917 at Varennes, and included in a letter to Scott dated 9 February 1917; another manuscript, dated 'Jan 1917', was included in a letter to her of 23 February. It is dedicated to F. W. Harvey (1888–1957), who Gurney feared had been killed while out on a raid. In fact, Harvey had wandered into the German trenches at Douai and been taken prisoner. He spent the rest of the war in seven camps including Gütersloh and Krefeld. Gurney met 'Will' Harvey at King's School, Gloucester and the two were close friends. Harvey wrote verse as a schoolboy and 'there can be no doubt that it was his example that first set Gurney on the poet's path' (Hurd, p. 24). 'Ypres – Minsterworth' is also dedicated to Harvey.

2. *With tea-talk loud*: An echo perhaps of Rupert Brooke's 'Dining Room Tea' from his *Poems* (1911).

Requiem

Probably written in November 1916, east of Laventie, this is one of three poems entitled 'Requiem' sent in an envelope to Scott dated 8 November 1916. The envelope also contained a number of other poems in manuscript, including 'Bach and the Sentry'.

2. *earth's outworn shell*: An echo perhaps of Yeats's 'Adam's Curse' (1902):

> And in the trembling blue-green of the sky
> A moon, worn as if it had been a shell
> Washed by time's waters as they rose and fell
> About the stars and broke in days and years.

Pain

Probably written in January or February 1917 at Crucifix Corner and included in the letter to Scott of 7 February 1917; this is the second sonnet in a sequence entitled 'Sonnets 1917 [To the memory of Rupert Brooke]' that ends *Severn & Somme*; the others are 'England', 'Servitude', 'Home-Sickness' and 'England the Mother'. Gurney asserted that 'they will make good antithesis; but note the rest will be quite different; this being the blackest' (Thornton, p. 203). The sequence was, he wrote,

> intended to be a sort of counterblast against [Brooke's] 'Sonnetts 1914', which were written before the grind of war and by an officer (or one who would have been an officer.) They are the protest of the physical against the exalted spiritual; of the cumulative weight of small facts against the one large. Of informed opinion against uninformed, (to put it coarsely and unfairly) and fill a place. Ladies won't like them, but soldiers may, and these things are written either for soldiers or civilians as well informed as the French what 'a young fresh war' means. (Or was it 'frische (joyful) Krieg'. I can't remember, but something like it was written by the tame Germans in 1914.) I know perfectly well how my attitude will appear, but – They will be called 'Sonnetts 1917' [. . .]
>
> (ibid., p. 210)

> Daniel Hipp points out how Gurney uses the repetition of the words 'pain' and 'grey' 'to give the sense of both the monotonous existence and seemingly endless exposure to and experience of human suffering' and how the sonnet form is a riposte to 'Brooke's war sonnets with their elevated diction, emblematic of the stage in the war before things got this ugly'.
>
> (pp. 120–21)

Servitude

Probably written in February 1917 and included in a letter to Scott dated 14 February 1917. It is the third sonnet in the sequence entitled 'Sonnets 1917 [To the memory of Rupert Brooke]'; see 'Pain' headnote above.

Turmut-Hoeing

Written in August 1918 at Hertford.

Title: 'Turmut' is dialect for turnip. The title of an English folk song, whose opening stanza runs:

'Twas on a jolly summer's morn, the twenty-first of May,
Giles Scroggins took his turmut hoe, with which he trudged away
For some delights in haymakin', and some they fancies mowin',
But of all the trades as I likes best, give I the turmut hoein'.

Ypres – Minsterworth

Written in July 1918 at Warrington.

Dedication: F. W. Harvey: see 'After-Glow' headnote above.

13–14 *in some German prison / A boy lies*: See 'After-Glow' headnote.

To His Love

Written in December 1917 at Seaton Delaval, Northumberland, where Gurney was on a signalling course; the manuscript is on army canteen paper. It was included in a letter to Scott dated 20 January 1918, but dated '1917' by Gurney which Thornton believed to be 'obviously a slip for 1918' (p. 398), and Hurd further suggests that the poem was 'sketched on the battlefield itself' as Gurney's reaction to hearing F. W. Harvey was presumed killed (p. 117): see 'After-Glow' headnote. Gurney's annotated copy of *War's Embers* gives the location of composition as Hertford.

Title: Recalls Christopher Marlowe's 'A Passionate Shepherd to His Love', but is also 'very much of the period and circumstances, a memorial in the innocent homoerotic overtones of war and comradeship' (Hurd, p. 117).

16. *Cover him, cover him soon*: An allusion to the revenge tragedies of John Webster: 'And with leaves and flowers do cover / The friendless bodies of unburied men' (*The White Devil* (1612), V, iv) and 'Cover her face; mine eyes dazzle: she died young' (*The Duchess of Malfi* (1623), IV, ii).

Photographs

Written in December 1917 at Seaton Delaval, Northumberland, and included in the same letter to Scott as 'To His Love' (see its headnote above). Gurney's annotated copy of *War's Embers* gives the location as Arras.

11. *Dicky-bird*: A small bird such as a canary, robin or sparrow; the term was often used by photographers who coaxed their sitters to 'watch the dicky-bird!'
24. *A girl who better had not been beloved*: Hurd suggests that 'in this poem there is an element of personal foreknowledge, for while in hospital Gurney had met and fallen in love with a V.A.D. nurse, Annie Nelson Drummond. She, however, had almost certainly not fallen in love with him' (p. 118). Gurney was in Edinburgh War Hospital, recovering from being gassed at St Julien in September 1917.

To the Prussians of England

Written in October 1917 at Bangour, and included in a letter to Scott dated 12 October 1917. Gurney revised the final original final couplet – 'We'll have a word there too, and England's life / Is dear, and for her cancer forge a knife' – because Scott objected to it (Thornton, p. 349; Kavanagh, p. 366). Gurney wrote to her on 16 October:

> I am very sorry that you have taken the sonnet 'To the Prussians of England' as meant for yourself. That Sonnet was originally named 'To the Prussians of England the Evening Stump', which, being interpreted, is no more than the *Morning Post.* My dear friend, your frail body seems to me to have given you an over tender conscience. At present I agree with you that the ruling class of Germany shows no signs of repentance [. . .] (Thornton, p. 352)

11. *An armed Mistress, braggart of the tide*: A reference to Britannia, who 'ruled the waves', as personified in the poem 'Rule Britannia' by James Thomson (1700–1748), which was set to music in 1740 by Thomas Arne, and came to be regarded as an unofficial national anthem.

Crickley Hill

Written in July 1918 while Gurney was a patient at Lord Derby's War Hospital, Warrington. He wrote on 27 August 1918 to Scott that 'The irregular rhyme scheme was a mistake. "You" and "dew" are not perfect rhymes, but will pass without any notice among the critics' (Thornton, p. 443). In another letter to Scott of *c.* 21 September 1918 he said: ' "Crickley Hill" I must have a shot at later, for certainly as

Mr Haines says the later part is too rhetorical' (ibid., p. 463). John Wilton Haines was a solicitor with a particular interest in poetry, who knew many of the Georgian poets including Robert Frost, Edward Thomas and Lascelles Abercrombie, as well as Gurney and Harvey. By 28 September Gurney had not progressed with the revisions: 'the fact is the whole thing needs making again if it is to be any good; and that needs really too much time, patience, and so forth to be done just at present' (ibid., p. 465). It may have been omitted from *War's Embers* by mistake (Kavanagh, p. 366). Edna Longley has dubbed it 'perhaps Gurney's most rapturous expression of local patriotism' (in Kendall (2007), p. 470).

Title: Crickley Hill, an important Neolithic site with an Iron Age hillfort, is located on the Cotswold scarp, overlooking the Vale of Gloucester.

1. *orchis, trefoil, harebells*: Wildflowers.
8. *Buire-au-Bois*: A small farming commune 40km west of Arras, in northern France, where Gurney and his battalion rested and trained in late June/early July 1917.

37–8 *still keep / Memory of us*: Cf. 'Song', line 7.

Between the Boughs

Written probably between 1919 and 1922. No MS is extent and the poem now exists only in typescript.

If I Walked Straight Slap

Written sometime between 1917 and 1919 in a notebook Gurney carried on a walking tour of the Black Mountains with John Haines in August 1919. The whereabouts of the notebook is now unknown, and the poem exists only in typescript.

The Valley Farm

Written between 1919 and 1922 and copied into a black exercise book inscribed 'I. Gurney, Westfield Terrace, Longford, Gloucester', which was subsequently sent to Edward Marsh in 1922.

6–7 *the Fortunate / Or fabled islands*: The Greeks and Romans believed these to be where the souls of the virtuous or blessed went after death.

I Saw England – July Night

Written between 1919 and 1922 in the black exercise book (see 'The Valley Farm' headnote above).

13. *Will Squele*: The name of the 'Cotswolds man' in Shakespeare's 2 *Henry IV* (III, ii).
14. *Edward Thomas*: See 'The Mangel-bury', line 1 and note.
15. *Borrow . . . heights*: George Borrow (1803–1881) and Thomas Hardy (1840–1928); *Sussex tales out of Roman heights*: Probably Kipling's *Puck of Pook's Hill* (Kavanagh, p. 369).

When March Blows

Written between 1919 and 1922 in the black exercise book (see 'The Valley Farm' headnote above). There is another copy in a marbled notebook with slightly different punctuation and word choice.

3. *meres*: Broad and shallow, small lakes.

Yesterday Lost

Written between 1919 and 1922 in the black exercise book (see 'The Valley Farm' headnote above). There is another manuscript version entitled 'The Miracles'.

3. *Bredon . . . Dursley*: A Worcestershire village and a town in Gloucestershire, respectively.

The Lock Keeper

Written between 1919 and 1922 in the black exercise book (see 'The Valley Farm' headnote above). An earlier version was dedicated to Edward Thomas and there are resonances of his 'Lob' in this poem. 'The flow of the rhyming couplets (with intermittent variations) permits accumulating detail and reflection, the impression of the copiousness of the lock-keeper's knowledge and that he encompasses in his single being the life and work and lore of a whole countryside' (Hugh Underhill, 'Ivor Gurney', *English Association Bookmarks*, no. 51 (2007), p. 4).

21. *tentaculous*: A variation (also line 88) on the adjective 'tentacular', meaning of the nature of a tentacle or tentacles.

27–8 *or a barge . . . The lowering of the waters, the quick inflow:* A reference to the lock system on canal waterways or rivers, in which boats are raised or lowered to navigate different levels of water. Locks are a particular feature of rivers in Oxfordshire and Gloucestershire.

34. *his line of fire:* An allusion to the straight sighting of a target, usually by a sniper with a rifle.

87. *kenning:* from the Anglo-Saxon, meaning 'to know'; '"Kenning" suggests a far back into the past of the land and of the people' (Underhill, 5). A 'Kenning' is also a compound metaphor from Anglo-Saxon and Old Norse poetry, e.g. 'whale-road' for 'sea'.

The Dearness of Common Things

Written between 1919 and 1922 in the black exercise book (see 'The Valley Farm' headnote above).

Title: Gurney may have had Rupert Brooke's poem 'The Great Lover' (1914) in mind.

4. *helves*: The handles of weapons or tools.

12. *worsted*: A lightweight, coarse wool cloth made from worsted yarn, but here denoting the texture of the clouds.

Water Colours

Written between 1919 and 1922. The typescript made by Marion Scott, which had minor alterations of punctuation was the version used by Blunden in his edition (see Note on the Texts), and is used here.

3. *cuckoo-flower*: Perennial wildflower (*Cardamine pratensis*) also known as Lady's Smock.

Laventie

Written between 1921 and 1922 in a green exercise book inscribed by Gurney as 'The Note Book (between music makings) of Ivor Gurney 1921–22, corrected Feb 1925, Ivor Gurney', from which the text is taken. Another manuscript version has the title 'Laventie Front'.

Title: Laventie was a village on the La Bassée Front, opposite Aubers Ridge and north-east of Béthune, in Artois. Over 800 war casualties are commemorated in the Royal Irish Rifles graveyard there. Eric Henri Kennington's painting, *The Kensingtons at Laventie, Winter 1914*, is credited as the first realistic portrayal of soldiers in the Great War. Gurney's Gloucester battalion was in reserve at Laventie in June 1916, and 'required only to bring in and bury the dead' (Hurd, p. 69). According to the battalion history, 'judged in the light of later experiences, the Laventie front was a peaceful spot and everyone was sorry to leave it' (quoted in ibid., p. 69). The poem is reminiscent of May Wedderburn Cannan's 'Rouen' (1917) for the ways in which it catalogues the everyday scenes of war.

12. *damning*: A play on words: plugging 'leaks in rainy times' ('damming') and swearing at the task.
16. *Tommies'*: 'Tommy' is short for Tommy Atkins, a name ascribed to the typical private soldier in the British army. It has its origins in the early nineteenth century, and was popularized by Kipling in his poem 'Tommy', published in *Barrack-Room Ballads* (1892).
17. *minnie werfs*: German trench-mortars.
19. *strafes*: Fierce assaults or attacks from low-flying aircraft.
22. *Heaven's gate:* Cf. Shakespeare's 'wonderful sweet air': 'Hark, hark! the lark at heaven's gate sings' in *Cymbeline* (V, i, 38).
23. *Cooper's*: Cooper's Hill, Gloucestershire.
24. *Framilode*: A village by the Severn in Gloucestershire.

29–30 *Machonachie . . . Spiller and Baker*: Trench rations. Machonachie was a tinned meat and vegetable stew; Paxton, Tickler and Stephens were tinned jams; Fray Bentos, tinned meat, a brand still sold today. Such a 'roll-call' 'alchemizes trench rations into poetry' (Kendall (2006), p. 97).

35. *Stand-to*: Short for 'Stand-to-Arms', a daily routine observed by both sides morning and evening. Morning stand-to was an hour before dawn, with the company being ordered to take up their attack positions, bayonets fixed, to guard against a dawn raid; it came also to be known as 'morning hate'.
37. *Tilleloy, Fauquissart, Neuve Chapelle*: Towns in northern France, the sites of particularly bloody battles.

Half Dead

Written between 1921 and 1922 in the green exercise book (see 'Laventie' headnote above).

4. *body-creepers*: Lice.
6. *Witcombe Steep*: Witcombe is a village in the Cotswolds.
8. *cloths of heaven*: Cf. Yeats's 'He wishes for the cloths of Heaven' (1899).
9. *Sirius . . . those seven*: Sirius, or the Dog Star, is the brightest star in the night sky. Mars, the 'Red planet' named after the Roman god of war. Argo, the ship in which Jason and his Argonauts sailed to retrieve the Golden Fleece, the namesake of the constellation Argo Navis. 'Pleiads, or Pleiades, is a cluster of bright blue stars in the constellation of Taurus named after the daughters of Atlas and Pleione in Greek mythology: Merope, Electra, Maia, Taygete, Celaeno and Alcyone.
11. *Cranham*: A village in the Cotswolds, near Gloucester.
16. *Caulaincourt's Mausoleum*: 'Memorable for its ruined chateau, and a mausoleum, unaccountably left intact, in which two companies of Gloucesters (one being Gurney's) decided to make their billet' (Hurd, pp. 95–6).
21. *Regulus*: The brightest star in the constellation Leo.

Crucifix Corner

Written between 1921 and 1922 in the green exercise book (see 'Laventie' headnote above).

Title: High Wood (Bois des Fourcaux, or on maps in the First World War, Bois des Foureaux), a small forest near Bazentin le Petit in the Somme region of northern France, was one of the last places to be taken by the British in the Somme offensive of 1916. Nearly 8,000 British soldiers' remains are interred there. 'Crucifix Corner' was the name given to many road junctions on the Western Front that had a wayside crucifix, a common feature of the French countryside. The original High Wood Crucifix remains to this day, battered with holes.

3. *Those rolling tanks . . . mixture*: Sanitation tankers, thus not the same as the 'Tanks' referred to in 'War Books', line 19.
5. *Aveluy*: A town in Picardy, northern France.
10. *Noel*: Christmas.
15. *Last Trump*: 1 Corinthians 15:52.
17. *Hundred Pipers and A'*: An old Scottish folk song, the authorized March of the 49th (Sault-Ste-Marie) Field Artillery.
22. *Orion and the seven stars*: The constellation of Orion, the Hunter in Greek mythology, is made up of seven major stars and can be seen in the northern hemisphere in autumn and winter.

The phrase has biblical allusions, especially Amos 5:8: 'Seek him that maketh the seven stars and Orion, and turneth the shadow of death into the morning, and maketh the day dark with night: that calleth for the waters of the sea, and poureth them out upon the face of the earth: The LORD is his name.'

27. *Sir Walter*: Sir Walter Scott (1771–1832), Scottish novelist, author of *The Antiquary* (1816); *The Heart of Midlothian* (1818); *Redgauntlet* (1824).
29. *Solway*: The firth that forms part of the border between Scotland and Cumbria.

Strange Hells

Written between 1921 and1922 in a pink marbled exercise book, as are the following seven poems.

8. *tin and stretched-wire tinkle*: Barbed wire.
9. *Après la guerre fini*: After the war is over (French); this familiar catchphrase came to mean 'never', jokingly used for a remote future, and more seriously in a resigned sense that the end of the war was remote. A popular song put the phrase into another context: 'Après la guerre fini, / Anglais soldats parti, / Mademoiselle in the family way, / Après la guerre fini.'
11. *State-doles*: Welfare payments or charity meted out by the government.
12. *tatterns*: Rags or old, worn and 'tattered' clothes.

After War

Written between 1921 and 1922 in the pink marbled exercise book (see 'Strange Hells' headnote above).

2. *the straps slipped*: Taking off packs after a march.

Near Vermand

Written between 1921 and 1922 in the pink marbled exercise book (see 'Strange Hells' headnote above). Another poem with the same title begins: 'A park there with a stream running, deep up-and-down / Banks sliding with green face, and young trees running hither / And thither in the small valley'. Gurney's company of the Gloucesters reached the village of Vermand on 31 March 1917, attacking and clearing the village of Bihecourt two days later (Hurd, p. 96).

1. *clutch-frost*: Fierce frost that 'clutched' at earth and flesh.
5. *spinnies*: A spinney is a small wood or copse.

Early Spring Dawn

Written between 1921 and 1922 in the pink marbled exercise book (see 'Strange Hells' headnote above).

First Time In

Written between 1921 and 1922 in the pink marbled exercise book (see 'Strange Hells' headnote above). Another poem entitled 'First Time In' begins: 'The Captain addressed us, the afterglow grew deeper – / West Country light'.

5. *Soft foreign things*: Refers to the language of the soldiers of the 'Welsh colony' (line 3).
14. *Ulysses*: Or Odysseus, the legendary Greek king of Ithaca and hero of Homer's epic poem *The Odyssey*.
15. *'David of the White Rock', the 'Slumber Song'*: Welsh songs. In a letter to Scott, dated 7 June 1916, Gurney wrote:

> these few days in the signal dugout with my Cymric friends are of the happiest for years [. . .] Yesterday in the trenches [. . .] [t]here was a trench mortar strafe, and we had casualties. As I was in Signallers' dugout, a bombardment missed me and a tin of Machonachie (my dinner) by ten yards; a shower of dirt, no more. Good luck to us all. I have been told that I may say that we are with the Welsh. They sang David of the White Rock and the Slumber Song, both of which Somerville has arranged. And O their voices! I thank God for the experience [. . .]
>
> (Thornton, p. 87)

16–17 *to which roguish words . . . Are sung*: Soldiers often remade songs and especially hymns by applying bawdy words to traditional melodies.

Behind the Line

Written between 1921 and 1922 in the pink marbled notebook (see 'Strange Hells' headnote above). There is also a typescript with Gurney's revisions, made in 1924, in which line 9 ends 'and the great' with 'great' crossed out and 'plain' inserted; it is possible that 'great' was a mistranscription of 'queer'.

4. *Robecq*: A commune in the Pas-de-Calais *département* of the Nord-Pas-de-Calais region of France.
5. *estaminets*: Small cafés.

Old Dreams

Written between 1921 and 1922 in the pink marbled notebook (see 'Strange Hells' headnote above). Gurney's 1924 revision to the typescript adds a third stanza.

The Not-Returning

Written between 1921 and 1922 in the pink marbled notebook (see 'Strange Hells' headnote above).

6. *Westward, Westward*: Perhaps an allusion to the euphemism 'go west', meaning to die.

Towards Lillers

Written between 1921 and 1922 in the pink marbled notebook (see 'Strange Hells' headnote above); a typescript corrected by Gurney also survives. The final two stanzas in the notebook are made a separate poem by Gurney in the typescript and entitled 'Aeroplanes over Aubers'.

Title: Lillers is the centre of a small region in northern France called Lillerois, bordered on the north by the river Lys.

7. *thirsty frames*: Bodies.
9. *estaminets*: Small cafés.
32. *Marathon*: Ancient Greek city-state. In the Battle of Marathon in 490 BC, an Athenian army of 10,000 defeated a Persian invasion force of over 20,000 infantry and cavalry; it is one of the first recorded battles in history.

Sonnet – September 1922

Typescript by Marion Scott.

3. *filed*: Short for 'defiled', sullied.
6. *rood*: The cross on which Christ suffered.

7. *poppy's blood*: The red of Flanders poppies was deemed to be the result of the blood of slaughtered soldiers.
9. *the toad under the harrow*: Kavanagh (p. 378) cites a suggestion from Barry Webb that this may refer to Kipling's epigraph to 'Paget MP', in *Departmental Ditties* (1885):

> The toad beneath the harrow knows
> Exactly where the toothpoint goes;
> The butterfly upon the road
> Preaches contentment to that toad.

14. *November keeps the guy*: Guy Fawkes's Night is commemorated on 5 November. Executed for treason for his part in the Gunpowder Plot in 1606, Fawkes is often referred to as 'the guy'.

The Incense Bearers

Written in early April 1923, the manuscript is inscribed in the upper right-corner: 'To the London Metropolitan Police', and signed 'I.B. Gurney'.

To God

Written in December 1922 (see 'The Incense Bearers' headnote above).

9. *Forced meals . . . electricity*: Force-feeding and electric-shock therapy, respectively.
11. *orders*: 'Presumably military "Orders of the Day" intended' (Kavanagh, p. 378). Hurd comments that 'the best of his asylum poems [. . .] make terrible reading . . . They sound like the utterances of a man whose mind may perhaps have momentarily lost its balance, but who was now being driven, little by little, into a state of total insanity' (pp. 162, 163).

The Interview

Written in September 1923 (see 'The Incense Bearers' headnote above); this manuscript is inscribed: 'for Saturday Westminster [Gazette] Competition', 'Signed I.B. Gurney'.

16. *Reserve*: In reserve or a reserve trench, i.e. not in the front-line. Three parallel trenches faced the enemy: the front-line trench which bordered No Man's Land, the support trench and the reserve trench.

Hedger

Written in January 1923 (see 'The Incense Bearers' headnote above).

1. *A Major Concerto*: Mozart's Piano Concerto No. 23 in A Major, K488.
5. *laying*: Trimming a hedge by cutting the boughs half through, then bending them down and intertwining them so as to strengthen the fence formed by the hedge (*OED*). See line 19, 'hedge-layer'.
14. *bill*: An implement used for pruning, cutting wood, lopping trees, hedges, etc., having a long blade with a concave edge, often ending in a sharp hook. A hedging-bill is probably referred to here, as the form of 'bill' varies greatly in different localities (*OED*).

On Somme

Written in October 1922; the manuscript is in pencil.

After 'The Penny Whistle'

Written in October 1922.

Title: Kavanagh conjectures that Gurney used the title because the poem has a similar rhythm and tone to Edward Thomas's 'The Penny Whistle' (p. 379).

First Poem

Written in February 1925, on the front page of the pink marbled notebook entitled 'The Book of Five Makings. Feb. 1925 (in torture)'. This notebook was used for *'Best Poems' and 'The Book of Five Makings'* (1995), ed. Thornton and Walter.

To Long Island First

This poem is in a typescript entitled 'In Praise of Poets. Some Poems of the States', a number of which are dated March 1925; it was prepared by a typist of Ralph Vaughan Williams. This poem shows Gurney's deep engagement with Walt Whitman, and declaring himself 'a disciple' (Kavanagh, p. 130) of the Master, Gurney averred that the American poet was

> One of the greatest teachers [. . .] he among others has this enormous virtue – that when he has nothing to say, you may divine it a mile off. A marked copy may be read in half an hour; but oh, what gorgeous stuff it is [. . .]
>
> (Kavanagh, p. 41)

Along with '*War and Peace* & Shakespeare [. . .] & St Matthew & Wordsworth & Plutarch', Whitman was for Gurney 'a pretty complete diet – mental pabulum' (ibid., pp. 71–2). Hawlin (p. 40) argues that the poem was 'a paean, and clearly intended to act as the opening collection or sequence, probably . . . Gurney's very own *Leaves of Grass*'.

Title: Long Island is one of the boroughs of New York City and is located east of Manhattan.

3. *'Leaves of Grass'*: Walt Whitman published the 1st edition of 12 poems at his own expense in 1855. A second edition, with an additional 21 poems, was published in 1856; he continued to revise and publish.
6. *Roman Cotswold, Roman Artois war stations*: The Cotswolds in southern England and the Artois region of northern France were both occupied by the Romans with significant settlements.
19. *Virgil*: Roman poet (70–19 BC), who wrote the epic *The Aeneid* as well as the pastoral poems known as the *Eclogues* and the *Georgics*.

Walt Whitman

In the typescript of 'In Praise of Poets. Some Poems of the States' (see 'To Long Island First' headnote above).

8. *Paumanok . . . kisses*: Paumanok is located on Long Island. Whitman was born on Long Island in 1819 and wrote a number of poems about Paumanok, including 'Starting from Paumanok' and 'A Paumanok Picture'; *son of responding kisses*: See Whitman's 'Vigil Strange I Kept on the Field' in *Leaves of Grass*.
12. *Bought of me . . . old Gloucester*: See lines 2–4 of 'To Long Island First'.

14–15 *'Song of Myself' . . . 'Calamus'*: Poems in *Leaves of Grass*.

Butchers and Tombs

Written in March 1925; only a typescript survives. 'The sonnet form emerges clearer and more meaningful from such refining fires' (Hurd, p. 203).

2. *Cotswold stone*: The distinctive yellow-coloured limestone quarried in the Cotswolds and used to build or face many of the region's buildings.
10. *ensign*: An emblem or badge.

The Bohemians

Written in March 1925; the poem exists in typescript only.

3. *putties*: Or 'puttees', a long strip of cloth or leather wound from the ankle to the knee for protection or support.

The Silent One

Written in late 1925 in the Asylum, in the notebook labelled 'Best Poems'. Another version exists in a second blue 'Marspen' exercise book, 1925.

3. *Bucks*: Buckinghamshire.
5. *stripes*: Chevron worn on the upper part of the coat-sleeve of a non-commissioned officer, such as a sergeant. A similarly shaped badge might also be worn by soldiers recognized for good conduct or by those wounded (*OED*).
17. *screen*: A contrivance to ward off heat from a fire, 'the screen is a thin boundary separating a world where speech ends as the silent one hangs dead on the wires, and a world of insanely finicking manners where lives are preserved and lost according to the ability to resist the expected etiquettes' (Tim Kendall, 'Ivor Gurney's Memory', *Modern English War Poetry* (Oxford, 2006), p. 100).

War Books

Written in late 1925 in the Asylum, in the notebook labelled 'Best Poems'.

10. *Corbie Ridge . . . Gonnehem*: Corbie is a small town 15 km south-west of Albert and approximately 23 km due east of Amiens, in the Somme Valley, northern France. Siegfried Sassoon also wrote of Corbie Ridge in 'Two Hundred Years On', *The Old Huntsman and Other Poems* (1918):

> Trudging by Corbie Ridge one winter's night,
> (Unless old hearsay memories tricked his sight)
> Along the pallid edge of the quiet sky
> He watched a nosing lorry grinding on [. . .]

Gonnehem is a village about 7 km north-west of Bethune and 7 km east of Lillers in northern France. In the middle of April 1918 the German front-line came within 3.2 km of the village.

11. *Fauquissart*: A hamlet near the town of Laventie, near Armentières, in northern France.
19. *Tanks*: The armoured fighting vehicles first developed and used by the British in the First World War. Cf. 'Crucifix Corner', line 3 and note.
20. *love came sweet in hospital*: Possibly a reference to Gurney's unrequited love for nurse Annie Drummond: see 'photographs', line 24 and note.

The Mangel-bury

Written in late 1925 in the Asylum, in the notebook labelled 'Best Poems'. An entirely different version is contained in the 'Marspen' exercise book (see also 'The Silent One').

Title: A thatch used to cover the mangel-wurzels, a variety of beet, being stored for cattle-food.

1. *Edward Thomas had fallen at Arras*: (Philip) Edward Thomas (1878–1917) was killed at the battle of Arras in April 1917. He enlisted in the army 1915, and between 1915 and 1917 some poems were published under his pseudonym, Edward Eastaway, though most were published posthumously. Edna Longley calls 'The Mangel-bury' 'perhaps Gurney's finest poem and one of his several poetic tributes to Edward Thomas, brings the trenches back home by updating Thomas's "Swedes"' (Kendall (2007), p. 472).

Farewell

Written in 1924 in the Asylum.

2. *Blighty*: See 'Ballad of the Three Spectres', note to line 8.
5. *frore:* Frozen or frosty.
30. *They bruise my head*: The effects of electric-shock therapy.
32. *the unbroken wires:* See 'The Silent One', line 4.

It is Near Toussaints

Written in 1924 in the Asylum. Tim Kendall has argued that the poem 'lapses into doggerel . . . , distorts word order to deliver rhymes . . . , and indulges in the blandest of imprecations . . . That the poem survives these calamities is testament to the strenuous force of a poetic language' (Kendall, 'Ivor Gurney's Memory', p. 93).

Title: La Toussaint is All Saints Day, celebrated on 1 November.

11. *Hilaire Belloc*: Writer and historian (1870–1953), military correspondent for *Land and Water*, which focused exclusively on the war effort and for which he wrote a weekly column.
13. *Pray Michael, Nicholas, Maries*: Ancient churches in Gloucester, including St Mary de Lode, St Mary Crypt and St Mary Magdalene.
16. *no bon*: No good! (French).

An Appeal for Death

Written in *c.* 1924–5 in the Asylum; the poem exists only in typescript. See Thornton, especially the letters of November and December 1922. Gurney wrote to Marion Scott, 'Death would be a rest from torment' (ibid., p. 546); to the Dean of Gloucester, 'The mercy of Death is continually desired' (ibid., p. 548); and to Sydney Scott, 'Grant sacred Mercy of death' (ibid., p. 549).

Hell's Prayer

Written in *c.* 1925–6 in the Asylum; the poem exists only in typescript.

11. *gages*: A gage is a pledge to do battle in support of one's assertions, usually in the form of a glove thrown on the ground, a challenge (*OED*).

December 30th

Written in *c.* 1925–6 in the Asylum; the poem exists only in typescript.

11. *Lassington*: A town in Gloucestershire.
13. *'Lear'*: Shakespeare's play *King Lear*.

Poem for End

Probably written in *c.* 1925–6 in the Asylum; the poem exists only in typescript. Another typescript was used by Blunden and was presumably lost.

11. *the dead Master*: Perhaps Walt Whitman.

ISAAC ROSENBERG

Note on the Texts

Isaac Rosenberg published three pamphlets of his work: *Night and Day*, with 10 poems, in 1912; *Youth*, 22 poems, in 1915; and *Moses*, with 9 poems and a play, in 1916.[1] About 50 copies of the first were printed, about 100 of the second, and an unknown (but probably no larger) number of the third. Consequently, they are today rare books.

There have been several posthumous collections of his work. The first, *Poems by Isaac Rosenberg*, selected and edited by Gordon Bottomley, with an introductory memoir by Lawrence Binyon, appeared in 1922. It contained *Moses*, extracts from *The Unicorn* and 'Night and Day' and 56 poems (one of them, 'Killed in Action', wrongly attributed to Rosenberg). *The Collected Works of Isaac Rosenberg: Poetry, Prose, Letters and Some Drawings*, edited by Bottomley and Denys Harding, with a Foreword by Siegfried Sassoon, followed in 1937. This contained all the poems then known, many fragments, the plays, prose writings, some letters, and examples of Rosenberg's paintings and drawings, a Biographical Note, an Editorial Note and seven pages of commentary. That edition was reissued in 1949 as *The Collected Poems of Isaac Rosenberg*, without the prose, letters and illustrations.

The Collected Works of Isaac Rosenberg: Poetry, Prose, Letters, Paintings and Drawings, edited with an Introduction and Notes by Ian Parsons and a Foreword by Siegfried Sassoon, was published in 1979. Its contents were substantially the same as the 1937 volume, except for the addition of four new poems, more extensive notes and variants, a biographical chronology and some further reproductions of paintings. For twenty-five years this remained the standard edition, but in 2004 was superseded by *The Poems and Plays of Isaac Rosenberg*, edited by Vivien Noakes, undertaken – and to be welcomed – for four reasons:

> The unreliability of the published text of some of the poems; the problems that have arisen from the systems of ordering and dating of poems used in earlier editions; the inadequacy and inconsistency of the notes; and the need to make available to scholars previous unpublished drafts and variants.[2]

For this major edition – unlikely itself to be superseded – Noakes returned to the manuscripts in the British Library and the Imperial War Museum. She was the first to catalogue, order and make a systematic attempt to date the manuscripts in the latter, larger collection. The Introduction to her edition gives an exemplary account of this daunting task, and should be read not only by those interested in Rosenberg's poems, but also, more generally, by anyone interested in recent advances in textual editing.

The texts of Noakes's 2004 edition became the copy-texts of her *Isaac Rosenberg*, now the standard 'readers' edition' of the poems and all his known letters, published in 2008, with a selection of black-and-white reproductions of the paintings and drawings. The editors of the present selection of Rosenberg's poems are grateful to Dr Noakes for permission to use her texts as their copy-texts.

In 1995, the manuscripts of 34 Rosenberg letters (all published in Noakes's 2008 edition) and 18 draft poems were rediscovered in the course of the British Library's removal from the British Museum. These were edited by one of the poet's biographers, Jean Liddiard. Entitled *Isaac Rosenberg: Poetry Out of My Head and Heart*, they were published in 2007 but their texts, it has to be said, are less accurate than those of Noakes's *Isaac Rosenberg* (2008).

NOTES

1. For a fuller bibliographical account of these – including lists of contents – see 'Publication History of Rosenberg's Works', in Noakes, pp. XV–XXXV and 417–18.
2. Ibid., p. XVI.

Ode to David's Harp

Written some time before 26 September 1905, this is thought to be Rosenberg's earliest surviving poem (Noakes, p. 300). He had sent it and others to Morley Dainow, Librarian of the Whitechapel Library, who on the 26th responded: 'I should not advise you to write so much. Only write when you are inspired & then arises such poems as the "Harp of David" and "The Charge of the Light Brigade"' (ibid.). From 1900 and perhaps earlier, Rosenberg had enthusiastically been reading Byron, whose 'The Harp the Monarch Minstrel Swept' (*Hebrew Melodies* (1815)) is the principal influence behind 'Ode to David's Harp'. David became the second king of Israel around 1000 BC.

Title: This, like the source of the poem, is taken from 1 Samuel: 16–19, 23 and 2 Samuel 6:5.

4. *Judah's barren shore*: Judah, name of an ancient Hebrew kingdom on the east coast of the Mediterranean. Cf. Byron, 'The Wild Gazelle' (line 1): 'The wild gazelle on Judah's hills'.

25–6 *Hark . . . burning fire*: Cf. Shelley, 'To a Skylark' (lines 1–5):

> Hail to thee, blithe Spirit!
> Bird thou never wert,
> That from Heaven, or near it,
> Pourest thy full heart
> In profuse strains of unpremeditated art.
>
> Higher still and higher
> From the earth thou springest
> Like a cloud of fire [. . .]

Raphael

Written probably in, or shortly after, the winter of 1911–12 when, in his notes for a proposed article on 'The Pre-Raphaelite Exhibition', Rosenberg

> recalled the foundation of the [Pre-Raphaelite] Brotherhood, where one of those gathered spoke 'of the correct soulnessness of Raphael – "O, if he hadn't lived"; then art had continued uninterrupted – of the crying need of a return to the men before Raphael'. IR's own sympathy was more with the PRB than with the Italian High Renaissance.
>
> (Noakes, p. 318)

'Raphael' shows in its structure, diction and punctuation, the strong influence of Browning's 'Andrea Del Sarto'. It seems likely that Rosenberg's title smuggles into his poem the name of his own silent interlocutor, a beloved model, who takes the place of Andrea Del Sarto's Lucrezia in Browning's dramatic monologue. A close friend and fellow immigrant, Annetta Raphael, worked as a dressmaker but studied painting at night: 'a few years older than Rosenberg, lovely, sensitive, and a little awkward, [she] must be considered as the most likely person to have initiated Rosenberg into sexual experience. [. . .] When she was told that [he] had been killed at the Front she suffered a nervous breakdown' (Cohen, p. 48).

Title: Raphael (1483–1520), painter of the Italian High Renaissance, whose classicism was admired by the European academic tradition.

33. *Limned*: Painted.
43. *Mighty Angelo*: Michelangelo (1475–1564), Italian Renaissance painter, poet and sculptor, featured with 'Rafael' in 'Andrea Del Sarto'.
46. *Jove's Thunders*: Jove, also known as Jupiter, chief of the Roman gods, was thought to wield the thunderbolt.
71. *elatement mayhap*: Elation perhaps.
96. *effable*: Capable of expression in words.

Dust Calleth to Dust

Probably written in 1912 (Noakes, p. 322), this poem draws, generally, on the Anglican 'Order for the Burial of the Dead': 'earth to earth, ashes to ashes, dust to dust'; and line 1, specifically, on Francis Thompson, 'An Anthem of Earth' (line 259): see 'Dead Man's Dump', note on lines 21–5.

On Receiving News of the War: Cape Town

Written between 24 August 1914, when snow fell on Table Mountain, and February 1915, when Rosenberg left Cape Town to return to England, this poem resembles such other writings of the day as Owen's '1914' (see p. 77) that foresaw an exhausted civilization cleansed and rejuvenated by blood-sacrifice, as Christ's crucifixion was believed to '[take] away the sins of the world' (Noakes, pp. 83–4).

The Dead Heroes

Written in autumn 1914 in South Africa (Noakes, p. 335), this poem with its three references to 'England' is hardly less patriotic than Brooke's sonnet 'The Soldier' (with six references to 'England/English'); and, with its echo of Blake's *Milton*, it invites comparison with Wilfred Owen's letter to his mother of December 1914: 'Do you know what would hold me together on a battlefield?: The sense that I was perpetuating the language in which Keats and the rest of them wrote!' (Owen and Bell, p. 300). Equally, it invites contrast with Rosenberg's 'Dead Man's Dump'.

6. *burning spears*: Cf. Blake, Prefatory stanzas to *Milton* (lines 9-12):

> Bring me my Bow of burning gold,
> Bring me my Arrows of desire,
> Bring me my Spear; O clouds unfold!
> Bring me my Chariot of fire!

At Sea-Point

Written between June 1914 and February 1915 in South Africa (Noakes, p. 338), this elegy for lost love may refer to a broken relationship with Margueretha Van Hulsteyn, a colourful actress 'younger than Rosenberg and equally small, [. . .] a striking figure, particularly in conservative Cape Town' (Moorcroft Wilson, pp. 217–22).

Title: Sea-Point is a well-known beauty spot near Cape Town.

1. *crumble away*: Cf. 'Break of Day in the Trenches', line 1.

God Made Blind

Written in late 1914 or early 1915 in South Africa, this must be the poem to which Rosenberg refers in his undated letter (of Spring 1915) to Edward Marsh:

> The idea in the poem I like best I should think is very clear. That we can cheat our malignant fate who has devised a perfect evil for us, by pretending to have as much misery as we can bear, so that it withholds its greater evil, while under that guise of misery there is secret joy. Love – this joy – burns and grows within us trying to push out to that. Eternity without us which is Gods heart. Joy – love, grows in time too vast to be hidden from God under the guise of gloom. Then we find another way of cheating God. Now through the very joy itself. For by this time we have grown into love, which is the rays of that Eternity of which God is the sun. We have become God Himself. Can God hate and do wrong to Himself?
>
> I think myself the poem is very clear, but if by some foul accident it isn't, I wonder if you see that idea in it.
>
> (Noakes, pp. 340–41)

1. *God-guiling*: God deceiving person.

5–8 *our joy . . . hidden in bed*: Cf. Blake, 'The Sick Rose' (lines 2–8):

The invisible worm [. . .]

Has found out thy bed
Of crimson joy,
And his dark secret love
Does thy life destroy.

The Blind God

Like 'God Made Blind' (see headnote above), to which it is clearly related, this was also written in 1914 or 1915 in South Africa (Noakes, p. 342).

4. *dreamless sleep*: Cf. Phillips Brooks, 'O Little Town of Bethlehem' (lines 3–4): 'Above thy deep and dreamless sleep / The silent stars go by'.

Wedded [II]

Written in 1914 or 1915 in South Africa (Noakes, p. 380), this has little in common with the markedly inferior 'Wedded I' (ibid., pp. 24 and 328–9), probably written in early 1914. The two poems may have been inspired by the marriage, the previous August, of Rosenberg's eldest sister, Minnie (Moorcroft Wilson, p. 197).

God

Written probably in 1915 (Noakes, p. 343), this incorporates lines 11–15 published in Rosenberg's play *Moses* in 1916 (ibid., pp. 202–3), and can be seen as

> his culmination poem on the theme of his rejection of God; it goes back to and incorporates the ideas he struggled with in 'Creation', his admiration for Coleridge's 'Sole Positive of Night', his successively defined image of the baleful God in 'Spiritual Isolation', 'The Blind God', 'The One Lost', 'Invisible Ancient Enemy of Mine', and 'God Made Blind'.
>
> (Cohen, p. 140)

3. *rat*: Cf. 'Break of Day in the Trenches', lines 3–18.

Marching – as seen from the left file

Written in late December 1915 at Bury St Edmunds, this is the first poem Rosenberg is known to have composed after he had enlisted at the end of October. He told Sydney Schiff in an undated letter, enclosing a typescript of the poem: 'I have written two poems ['Spring 1916' and 'Marching – as seen from the left file'] since I joined & I think they are my strongest work. I sent them to one or two papers as they are war poems & topical but as I expected, they were sent back. I am afraid my public is still in the womb' (Noakes, pp. 354–6). Rosenberg sent Ezra Pound a copy of his pamphlet *Moses*, in which 'Marching – as seen from the left file' and 'Break of Day in the Trenches' were first printed, and Pound passed it on to Harriet Monroe, who published both poems in the December 1916 issue of *Poetry* (Chicago).

10. *Mars*: Roman God of War.

'A worm fed on the heart of Corinth'

Written probably in May or early June 1916, before leaving England for France on 3 June (Noakes, p. 357), 'this prophecy of the fall of empire ranks perhaps highest among Rosenberg's visionary fragments' (F. Kermode and J. Hollander, *The Oxford Anthology of English Literature*, vol. 2 (1973), p. 2058).

1–2 *Corinth, / Babylon and Rome*: Powerful imperial cities, which fell partly as a result of inner corruption.

3. *Paris*: Son of Priam, king of Troy, whose abduction of Helen, wife of Menelaus, king of Sparta, led to the ten-year siege of Troy.

6. *amorphous sleep*: 'may be understood as England's self-hypnosis of wealth and power, the sick romanticism of imperial duty and sacrifice' (Geoffrey Hill, 'Isaac Rosenberg, 1890–1918', in *Collected Critical Writings*, ed. Kenneth Haynes (2008), p. 457).

9. *the shadowless*: The worm of death.

10. *Solomon*: Great and wealthy king of Israel (10th century BC), famously visited by the queen of Sheba (1 Kings 10).

In the Trenches

Written in June 1916 in France, this poem formed the second part of a letter, sent in July 1916 to Sonia Cohen (Noakes, *Rosenberg*, pp. 302 and 427). It was later substantially revised as 'Break of Day in the Trenches' (see headnote below).

Break of Day in the Trenches

Written in June 1916 in France, a fair copy was enclosed in a letter to Gordon Bottomley, postmarked 12 July 1916, who replied to Rosenberg:

'Thank you for the deeply interesting poems you send. I am glad to have them. [. . .] "In the Trenches" is the most completely good; it falls away a little at the end, but I like it ever so much.' In his next letter he said: 'Your sister very kindly sent me the revision of your Rat poem. [. . .] I thought the end was greatly improved, and I felt it ran straight along quite clearly and in a good shape' (Noakes, p. 360). Rosenberg sent a revised fair copy to Edward Marsh with an accompanying letter, dated 4 August [1916], in which he said: 'I am enclosing a poem I wrote in the trenches, which is surely as simple as ordinary talk. You might object to the second line as vague, but that was the best way I could express the sense of dawn' (ibid., p. 359). See Noakes, *Rosenberg*, p. 107, for a photograph of the complete typescript with pencilled corrections. See also headnotes to 'In the Trenches' and 'Marching – as seen from the left file'.

1. *crumbles away*: Cf. 'At Sea-Point', line 1.
2. *Druid Time*: Time personified as a priestly officer of pre-Roman Britain, believed to make human sacrifices at dawn. Rosenberg implies an analogy with 'sacrifices' routinely made in the dawn attacks that were a dreaded feature of the Western Front.
5. *parapet's poppy*: Cf. 'In the Trenches', lines 1–2.
7. *Droll rat*: Cf. Rosenberg, 'A flea whose body shone like lead' (line 5; Noakes, p. 95): 'A rat whose droll shape would dart and flit'.

9–10 *this English hand / You will do the same to a German*: Cf. John Donne, 'The Flea' (line 3): 'It sucked me first, and now sucks thee.'

22. *What quaver – what heart aghast*: Cf. Blake, 'The Tyger' (lines 9–12):

> And what shoulder, and what art,
> Could twist the sinews of thy heart?
> And when thy heart began to beat,
> What dread hand? And what dread feet?

23–4 *Poppies whose roots . . . ever dropping:* Cf. George Herbert, 'Virtue' (lines 5–8):

> Sweet rose, whose hue angry and brave
> Bids the rash gazer wipe his eye:
> Thy root is ever in its grave,
> And thou must die.

August 1914

Written in Summer 1916 in France, this poem was enclosed in an undated letter to Mrs Herbert Cohen (Noakes, pp. 360–61; Noakes, *Rosenberg*, p. 304).

7–8 *The gold, the honey gone . . . cold*: Death. Cf. 'Dead Man's Dump', lines 30–31.

The Dying Soldier

Written in France, but when is unknown (Noakes, p. 361).

The Immortals

Written in France, but when is unknown (Noakes, pp. 362–3) – this poem shares its subject with 'Louse Hunting' (see its headnote below).

15. *Balzebub*: Beelzebub, 'the prince of the devils' (Matthew 12:24).

Louse Hunting

Written between summer 1916 and February 1917 in France, this poem shares its subject with 'The Immortals' (see headnote above): it is not known which was written first.

> The [one] manuscript demonstrates most clearly the conditions under which [Rosenberg] was writing at the front. It is written with a soft pencil on bad quality paper which has been folded in four and is muddy and torn, especially down the right-hand side. It exists only in a very rough draft, and is the most difficult of his works to transcribe. No text can be final.
>
> The first mention of the thoughts for this poem come in a letter to [Bottomley] postmarked 23 July 1916: 'Last night we had a funny hunt for fleas. All stripped by candlelight, some Scots dancing over the candle burning the fleas, and the funniest, drollest and dirtiest songs and conversations ever imagined. Burns "Jolly Beggars" is nothing to it.' On 8 August 1916 [Bottomley] wrote to [Rosenberg]: 'I thought your Flea Hunt was a great subject; you must cherish it and carry it through. If I were you I should not tell too many poets about it, or certainly one of them will not be able to keep his hands off it. I find it difficult to resist it.' [Rosenberg] planned not only a poem but also a drawing of the subject; in a letter postmarked 17 September 1916 he told [Bottomley]: 'I must draw the "Flea hunt" if I don't write it.' He made a sketch of the scene, which he sent to [Bottomley], for on 19 March

1917 [Bottomley] wrote to thank him [...] Neither the earlier letter nor the drawing appears to have survived, and [Rosenberg] apparently did not send a finished copy of the poem to [Bottomley], who worked from this draft when preparing the *1922* edn. (Noakes, *Rosenberg*, pp. 385–6, which continues with an authoritative discussion of the manuscript's disputed readings).

Title: Cf. Robert Burns, 'To a Louse'.

13. *demons' pantomime*: Cf. Rosenberg, 'Night and Day' (line 204; Noakes, p. 53): 'Demons gurgling'.

From France

Written probably in 1916 in France (Noakes, p. 365).

9. *Heaped stones*: Traditionally, Jewish passers-by place a stone on a grave.
11. *And some birds sing*: Cf. Keats, 'La Belle Dame sans Merci' (line 4): 'And no birds sing.'

Returning, we hear the larks

Written in Spring 1917 in France, this poem recalls an undated prose piece, entitled 'Joy' (which Rosenberg had sent to Ruth Löwy in connection with his Slade Summer Competition entry for 1912, *Joy*, a painting of the same name that has not survived but is discussed in Moorcroft Wilson, pp. 153–5):

> And when we had seen Time die, and passed through the porches of silence, we came to a land where joy spread its boughs, and we knew that the dreams we had dreamed before Time were but the shadows of the tree of joy mirrored in the waters of life. For the roots of joy lie beyond the valleys and hills of life, and the branches thereof blossom where weeping earth mists come not near, and only the sounds of the laughing of ripples, the running of happy streams, and the rapturous singing of birds is heard. Where delight lies coolly shadowed, overburdened by the weariness of joy, lulled by the songs of joy. Joy – joy – the birds sing, joy – the rivers, joy – the happy leaves, for the fear of Time haunts not, and the hands of fate are afar.
>
> (Noakes, p. 366)

Title: Cf. Shakespeare, *Cymbeline*, II, iii, 22: 'Hark! Hark! The lark, at heaven's gate sings'; and Shelley, 'To a Skylark' (lines 1–5: see 'Ode to David's Harp', note to lines 25–6).

7–8 *But hark . . . unseen larks*: In 1912, Rosenberg entitled a charcoal and monochrome wash drawing 'Hark, hark, the lark' (reproduced in Cohen, p. 65).

10–12 *Death could drop . . . dropped*: Cf. Shelley, 'To a Skylark (lines 33–5):

> From rainbow clouds there flow not
> Drops so bright to see
> As from thy presence showers a rain of melody.

15–16 *a girl's dark hair . . . serpent hides*: Cf. Rosenberg, 'Knowledge' (lines 4–5; Noakes, p. 30): 'a despair / Lurks like a serpent hidden in his hair'.

Dead Man's Dump

Completed in its existing form by 14 May 1917, four months after Rosenberg's transfer to the Royal Engineers (Noakes, pp. 367–8, which gives a full account of the manuscript complexities). In a letter postmarked 8 May 1917, he told Marsh:

> Ive written some lines suggested by going out wiring, or rather carrying wire up the line on limbers & running over dead bodies lying about. I don't think what Ive written is very good but I think the substance is, & when I work on it Ill make it fine.
>
> (ibid., p. 368)

Marsh replied that he disapproved of mixing rhyme with free verse, to which Rosenberg responded, in a letter postmarked 27 May 1917:

> I liked your criticism of 'Dead man's dump'. Mr Binyon has often sermonized lengthily over my working on two different principles in the same thing & I know how it spoils the unity of a poem. But if I couldn't before, I can now, I am sure plead the absolute necessity of fixing an idea before it is lost, because of the situation its conceived in. Regular rhythms I do not like much, but of course it depends on where the stress & accent are laid. I think there is nothing finer than the vigorous opening of Lycidas for music; yet it is regular. Now I think if Andrew Marvell had broken up his rhythms more he would have been considered a terrific poet.
>
> (ibid.)

Writing to Bottomley, in a letter postmarked 31 May 1917, Rosenberg said: 'I wrote a poem about some dead Germans lying in a sunken road where we dumped our wire. I have asked my sister to send it to you, though I think it commonplace.' Bottomley responded on 29 June 1917:

> I like 'Dead Man's Dump' too [as well as 'Daughters of War']; it is more unequal, and in places it suggests that it has absorbed more raw material, 'neat', than it can assimilate. But in places it gets beyond that more completely than any other war poetry I have seen, and now and then – as in the two sections beginning 'What fierce imaginings' – you get the same astonishing and entrancing quality as in the other poem. This kind of quality is your high-water mark yet, so you must keep it up.
>
> (Noakes, p. 368)

1. *limbers*: Wheeled gun-carriages that transport guns or other materials (as, here, wire).

3. *crowns of thorns*: Like that with which Christ was crowned, as king of the Jews, before his crucifixion (Matthew 27:29).

4. *sceptres old*: In Matthew's account of the crucifixion, the soldiers put a reed (as sceptre) in Christ's right hand; but Rosenberg's principal allusion is to the legend of Canute the Great, eleventh-century king of Denmark and England, seated at the sea's edge, ordering the tide to obey his rule (represented by his sceptre) and retire.

11. *Man born of man, and born of woman*: Cf. Job 14:1: 'Man that is born of a woman'.

14. *Earth has waited*: Cf. Rosenberg, 'Death' (line 1; Noakes, p. 10): 'Death waits for me'.

21–5 *Earth! have they . . . God-ancestralled essences*: Cf. Francis Thompson, 'An Anthem of Earth' (lines 259–60, 262–3):

> In a little dust, in a little dust,
> Earth, thou reclaim'st us [. . .]
> Thou dost this body, this enhavocked realm
> Subject to ancient and ancestral shadows.

24. *soul's sack*: Cf. Rosenberg, *Moses* (line 102; Noakes, p. 190): 'Soul sack fall away'.

25. *God-ancestralled essences*: A manuscript, enclosed with Rosenberg's letter to Bottomley postmarked 23 June 1917, reads: 'Emptied of all that made the young lean Time / Eye with thief's eyes, shouldering his masters load / Of proud Godhead ancestralled essences'. Cf. Rosenberg, *'The Amulet'* (line 154; Noakes, p. 239): 'It mixes with all God-ancestralled essences'.

27–8 *their spirits' shadow shake the grass . . . to pass*: Cf. Rosenberg, 'The Mirror' (lines 5–6; Noakes, p. 93): 'No shade shall waver there when your shadowless soul shall pass, / The green shakes not the air when your spirit drinks the grass'.

27–9 *the grass . . . doomed mouth*: Cf. Psalm 103:15–16: 'As for man, his days are as grass: as a flower of the field, so he flourisheth. For the wind passeth over it, and it is gone; and the place thereof shall know it no more.'

30–31 *When the swift iron . . . honey of their youth*: Cf. 'August 1914', lines 5–10, and 'Death' (line 5; Noakes, p. 10): 'even the honey on life's lips is curst'.

34. *ichor*: In Greek mythology, the divine fluid flowing in the veins of the gods.

56–7 *Burnt black . . . faces lie*: Cf. Lamentations 4:8: 'Their visage is blacker than a coal', and Rosenberg, *The Amulet*, 'Tel's Song' (line 4, Noakes, p. 273): 'But thence a strange decay'.

63–70 *His dark hearing . . . his sight*: Cf. Wilfred Wilson Gibson, 'Wheels' (lines 3–5, 7–8, 35–7, 67–8):

> He tumbled heavily, but all unheard
> Amid the skurry of wheels that crashed and whirred
> About his senseless head [. . .]
> And as he lay
> He heard again the wheels he'd heard all day [. . .]
> And still within a hair's breadth of his ear
> The crunch and gride of wheels rings sharp and clear,
> Huge lumbering wagons, crusted axle-deep [. . .]
> and a roar
> Of wheels and wheels and wheels for evermore [. . .]
>
> (*New Numbers*, 1: 3 (August 1914))

64. *stretched weak hands*: Cf. Rosenberg, 'Dawn Behind Night' (line 8; Noakes, p. 7): 'outstretch the kind hand in relief'.

71. *Will they come*: Perhaps an echo of the slogan on an early recruiting poster, showing soldiers in action and in need of reinforcements: 'Will they never come?'

Daughters of War

This poem was begun probably in October 1916 in France, and completed there some time after June 1917. On an undated typescript of 'Returning, we hear the larks', that Rosenberg sent to John Rodker, he added: 'I will send you when I get it typed a poem I call Daughters of War, done in the grand style, but I think my best poem.' The first dateable reference occurs in a letter of 21 December 1916 from Bottomley, who wrote of an early draft:

> It has imperfections; but it contains more than one part of the new merit of which you speak, because in the best passages it attains a texture of a personal yet a high quality, and it nowhere fails in keeping up this texture completely. To produce a texture is not the purpose of art or its raison d'être, as the Imagist painters often think; yet they are so far right in that the achievement of a mysterious, inscrutable texture that justifies itself to a long-trained taste is the surest test as to whether a work of art has been achieved. [. . .] So I am sure your poem has elements of the best kind of beauty in it, because it has a remarkable, close-knit, firm, spare texture; and because the formation of the texture causes a feeling of music in the mind. It is unequal: it gathers strength as it goes on, and it is at its best at the end, where it is simple as well as complex. At the beginning it is not sure-footed, it is not certain of its direction.
>
> (Noakes, p. 371)

In a letter postmarked 31 May 1917, Rosenberg wrote: 'I've made it into a little book for you, as I like the poem.' 'This 6-page presentation copy is written on scraps of paper – parts of envelopes, part of page torn from a receipt book, part of a serrated sheet torn from a notebook – with the outer cover made from the outside of a Utopia Writing Tablet' (Noakes, *Rosenberg*, p. 391 and, for a photograph of page 6 of the presentation copy, 117. For a fuller account of the poem's genesis, see Noakes, pp. 369–74).

In the summer of 1917, Rosenberg told Bottomley of his disappointment that Marsh had selected an extract from *Moses*, not 'Daughters of War', for his anthology *Georgian Poetry, 1916-17*. Bottomley replied on 7 August 1917:

> I understand very well your wishing that 'Daughters of War' could go in too. It is your most remarkable poem for vision and originality and texture of language, and to me it gives the most certain promise of a fine future if you cultivate your talent and bring it completely within your own control. [. . .] If I were asked I could not deny that I thought 'Daughters of War' obscure; I could not, in fact always explain to anybody what it means.
>
> (Noakes, p. 373)

Title:

> An echo possibly of Ralph Waldo Emerson's 'Daughters of Time', in it Rosenberg signals his intention of creating his own mythology. Somewhere between the male war god of Classical legend and Odin's messenger maidens of Norse sagas, the Valkyries, the warlike 'Daughters' fulfil a role similar to their Scandinavian equivalents, whose special function is to kill the heroes selected by the gods for death in battle and conduct them to Valhalla. Rosenberg's warrior maidens, who also owe some of their attributes to the Amazons and to his own Female God, do not actually kill those destined to die in battle, but wait, even more sinisterly, to possess them in death, just as the Earth in 'Dead Man's Dump' 'waited' for the soldiers, 'fretting for their decay'.
>
> (Moorcroft Wilson, p. 359)

1. *ruddy*: Cf. 'The Jew,' line 5.
22. *Amazons*: In Greek mythology, a race of fierce female warriors.
38. *terrene*: Earthly.
42. *thewed*: Muscular.

The Jew

Written probably in summer 1917, when a pencil holograph of the poem was enclosed in a letter to Gordon Bottomley postmarked 11 July 1917 (Noakes, *Rosenberg*, pp. 392–3).

3. *Ten immutable rules*: The Ten Commandments given by God to Moses on Mount Sinai (Exodus 20:2–17, and Deuteronomy 5:6–21).

Girl to Soldier on Leave

Written in September or October 1917 in France, this – like other of Rosenberg's poems – demonstrates his anticipation of what T. S. Eliot, in his influential review of James Joyce's novel *Ulysses*, would call 'the mythic method':

> In using the myth, in manipulating a continuous parallel between contemporaneity and antiquity, Mr Joyce is pursuing a method which others must pursue after him. [. . .] It is simply a way of controlling, of ordering, of giving a shape and a significance to the immense panorama of futility and anarchy which is contemporary history.
>
> ('Ulysses, Order and Myth', *Dial*, November 1923)

See also 'Soldier: Twentieth Century' headnote.

1. *Titan*: A gigantic race, the children of Uranus and Gaea, in Greek mythology. The Titans fought a long war against Zeus, who defeated and expelled them from heaven. Joseph Leftwich remembered Rosenberg, around 1911, doing 'illustrations to his own poems and to other poems – a charcoal composition, for instance, illustrating a passage in Keats, depicting the Titans, some with masses of rock on their bodies, some strangling snakes' (*Jewish Chronicle*, Supplement, no. 167 (February 1936), p. ii).

6. *Prometheus*: The Titan who stole fire from Olympus for mankind, and was punished by being chained to Mount Caucasus. Every day an eagle devoured his liver, and every night it was renewed until at last he was released.

9. *Pallid days*: Cf. 'Soldier: Twentieth Century', line 9, and 'Through these pale cold days', line 1.

11. *Babel cities'*: See Genesis 11:3–4. A city of burnt brick, Babel was built by the descendants of Noah, with a tower designed to 'reach unto heaven'. For their presumption 'the Lord scattered them' and tower and city were abandoned.

13. *gyves*: Fetters or shackles.

15. *Circe's swine*: A sorceress, in Homer's *Odyssey*, who turned Odysseus's shipmates into swine (pigs).

17. *the Somme*: River and region of north-west France that gave its name to a major and murderous battle which began on 1 July 1916 and continued into 1917.

Soldier: Twentieth Century

Written probably in autumn 1917 in France (Noakes, p. 375), this poem would seem to be a development – even a later draft – of Rosenberg, 'Girl to Soldier on Leave'.

1. *Titan*: Cf. 'Girl to Soldier on Leave', line 1 and note.

5. *unthinkable torture*: Cf. Rosenberg, *The Unicorn* (lines 88–9; Noakes, p. 250): 'But God's unthinkable imagination / Invents new tortures for nature'.

14–15 *pallid days . . . Circe's swine'*: Cf. 'Girl to Soldier on Leave', lines 9 and 15, and note to line 15.

'Through these pale cold days'

Written in March 1918 in France, this is Rosenberg's last surviving poem (Noakes, p. 375). He enclosed it in a letter to Marsh on

28 March 1918, with the comment: 'Heres just a slight thing. [...] I've seen no poetry for ages now so you mustnt be too critical – My vocabulary small enough before is impoverished & bare'. He was killed four days later, on 1 April.

1. *pale cold days*: Cf. 'Girl to Soldier on Leave', line 9, and 'Soldier: Twentieth Century', line 14.
3. *three thousand years*: Saul became the first king of Israel around 1020 BC, and was succeeded by David.
7. *Hebron*: One of the holy cities of Israel, set in the Judean hills near Jerusalem.

WILFRED OWEN

Note on the Texts

Only five of Owen's poems were published in his lifetime: 'Song of Songs' in *The Hydra / Journal of the Craiglockhart War Hospital* and the *Bookman*; 'The Next War' in *The Hydra*; and 'Miners', 'Futility' and 'Hospital Barge' in the *Nation*. At his death on 4 November 1918, the remainder were in manuscript, only a few of which were fair copies, and even fewer dated. The task of the successive editors – Sassoon and Edith Sitwell (1920), Blunden (1931), Day Lewis (1963) and Stallworthy (1983) – has, therefore, been the ordering and transcription of manuscript drafts in an attempt to establish the poet's latest intentions. Day Lewis wrote of the editor's principal problem in his Introduction to Owen's *Collected Poems* (1963):

> it is not always possible to determine the order in which these drafts were composed. [... And since] it is not possible to date a great number of these poems, I have arranged them in a non-chronological order. Part One gives all the completed poems which are directly concerned with the war [...] In Part Two I have placed the poems on other subjects, or not primarily concerned with the war, together with some fragments. Part Three offers a selection of Owen's juvenilia and minor poems [...]

This, effectively, reversed their order of composition and gave a misleading impression of the poet's development.

The problem of dating and consequent ordering of drafts and poems was largely solved some years later by a comparison of sixteen watermarks, paper, ink and pencil shared by Owen's undated drafts and dated letters. The results of this analysis are set out in the

Introduction to *Wilfred Owen: The Complete Poems and Fragments*, edited by Jon Stallworthy (1983), an edition more elaborate than any previously undertaken for a twentieth-century poet in the English language. When so many of an author's texts are, of necessity, editorial constructions, a sceptical reader needs to see the raw material from which they are constructed. The edition is in two volumes, enabling readers to have text, notes and manuscript material before them at the same time. Poems and fragments are numbered in chronological sequence and ordered by date of final revision rather than the first composition. Since the text in each case is intended to reflect Owen's latest intentions, it would have been misleading to place the poems and fragments in a chronology determined by his earliest version. The successive stages of composition are detailed and dated in a footnote to each poem, followed by any information relevant to its biographical, historical and literary context. The first volume contains plain texts of all finished poems, each with its accompanying note; and the second volume, supporting manuscript material – in the form of typeset facsimile – for 110 poems that could be called finished and 67 fragments. Together, these more than double the 79 poems and fragments in the 1963 *Collected Poems*. The second volume concludes with a table detailing the paper sizes and watermarks of his manuscripts. Information contained in the last of these explains the rationale behind the dating or redating of drafts and the consequent need to revise previously published texts. (A fuller account of the 'book history' of Owen's poems can be found in Jon Stallworthy, 'Owen and his editors', *Survivors' Songs from Maldon to the Somme* (Cambridge, 2008), pp. 81-97.)

The copy text of the poems in this volume is that of Stallworthy's *The Complete Poems and Fragments*.

Uriconium

Written in July 1913 probably at Shrewsbury (Stallworthy, *Owen*, pp. 88–90; Stallworthy, p. 211), when Owen was twenty and two years before he joined the Army, there is a sense in which this is his first 'war poem'. He had been a fascinated explorer of the remains of Uriconium, the Roman city at Wroxeter, on the river Severn, east of Shrewsbury, which with its inhabitants had been destroyed by fire and sword *c.* AD 400. The first excavations were carried out in 1859-61, and the more important finds placed in the Shrewsbury Museum. Owen's ode owes much of its material to his copy of George Fox's

Guide to the Roman City of Uriconium (1911), and something of its manner to the poems of Sir Walter Scott.

15. *Wrekin's shade*: The Wrekin is a hill to the east of Shrewsbury, named – together with 'Uricon' – in A. E. Housman's poem 'On Wenlock Edge the wood's in trouble'.
20. *Stretton Hills*: In north Cheshire.
28. *shaw*: A small wood.
39. *Marmion*: Lord Marmion, hero of Scott's poem, *Marmion: A Tale of Flodden Field* (1808), was killed at the Battle of Flodden (1513).
60. *Samian*: From the Greek island of Samos.
65. *Cymry*: The Welsh, with whom Owen romantically associated himself.
70. *Vesuvius'*: Owen owned a copy of Edward Bulwer-Lytton's novel, *The Last Days of Pompeii* (1834), about the destruction of that city following an eruption of the volcano Vesuvius in 79 AD.
75. *Viricon*: Ancient spelling of Uricon.
91. *Was ever sorrow like to mine*: Cf. Herbert, 'The Sacrifice' (line 4): 'Was ever grief like mine?'

Inspection

Drafted in August 1917 at Craiglockhart War Hospital and completed in September (Stallworthy, pp. 240–41), this poem shows the influence of Siegfried Sassoon's *The Old Huntsman and Other Poems*, a collection published shortly after he had himself arrived at Craiglockhart in August (Stallworthy, *Owen*, pp. 204–22).

7. *the damnèd spot*: An ironical echo of Lady Macbeth's 'Out, damnèd spot!' (Shakespeare, *Macbeth*, V, i, 38). Her wish to remove the guilt of Duncan's murder further prompts the 'washing out [. . .] white-washed' metaphor of lines 12–15. The whitewashing of parade-ground kerbstones, etc., prior to inspection, was an aspect of barrack-life much resented by British troops.

With an Identity Disc

Drafted on the Western Front in March 1917, and revised in August–September of that year at Craiglockhart (Stallworthy, *Owen*, pp. 175–6;*

* This and subsequent figures in bold type indicate a photograph of a manuscript.

Stallworthy, pp. 241–4), this sonnet shows the influence of Shakespeare, Sonnet 104, beginning 'To me, fair friend, you never can be old', and Keats, 'When I have fears that I may cease to be'. A British soldier carried three identity discs on a cord round his neck. They bore his name and number, and if he died, one was sent to his next of kin.

2. *High in the heart of London*: Owen was thinking of an engraved plaque in the Poets' Corner of Westminster Abbey.
8. *Keats*: He is buried among cypress trees in the Protestant cemetery at Rome.

Anthem for Doomed Youth

Written in September–October 1917 at Craiglockhart (Stallworthy, *Owen*, pp. 217–21, 222; Stallworthy, pp. 249–51; and Stallworthy, *Survivors' Songs*, pp. 95–6, for the transcription of a newly discovered ms), this sonnet was revised there with Sassoon's help.

1–12 *passing-bells . . . girls'*: Owen was probably responding angrily to the anonymous Prefatory Note to *Poems of Today: An Anthology* (1916), of which he possessed the December 1916 reprint:

> This book has been compiled in order that boys and girls, already perhaps familiar with the great classics of the English speech, may also know something of the newer poetry of their own day. Most of the writers are living, and the rest are still vivid memories among us, while one of the youngest, almost as these words are written, has gone singing to lay down his life for his country's cause. [. . .] there is no arbitrary isolation of one theme from another; they mingle and interpenetrate throughout, to the music of Pan's flute, and of Love's viol, and the bugle-call of Endeavour, and the passing-bells of Death.

7. *choirs of wailing shells*: Cf. Keats, 'To Autumn' (line 27): 'Then in a wailful choir the small gnats mourn.'
12. *their pall*: Traditionally, the red, white and blue Union Jack served as a pall, draping the coffin of a British soldier. Owen imagines the many dead, buried on the Western Front without such a pall, each accorded the more permanent pall of a girl's pale forehead shrouding their memory. It had long been customary in the British Isles to draw down the front-room blinds, or close the curtains, of a household in mourning (line 14).

1914

This sonnet was drafted in late 1914 in France, where Owen was teaching, and revised either in October–November 1917 at Craiglockhart or between November 1917 and January 1918 at Scarborough (Stallworthy, *Owen*, p. 105; Stallworthy, pp. 270–71).

1. *Winter of the world*: Cf. Shelley, *The Revolt of Islam* (lines 3685–6): 'This is the winter of the world; – and here / we die.'
9. *Spring had bloomed*: Cf. Keats, 'To Autumn' (lines 23–5):

> Where are the songs of Spring? Aye, where are they?
> Think not of them, thou hast thy music too –
> While barred clouds bloom the soft-dying day.

11–12 *Autumn . . . rich with all increase*: Cf. Shakespeare, Sonnet 97 (line 6): 'The teeming autumn big with rich increase'.

From My Diary, July 1914

Drafted either in October–November 1917 at Craiglockhart or between November 1917 and January 1918 at Scarborough, this poem is a poignant recollection of Owen's last peacetime summer, spent at the Villa Lorenzo, outside Bagnères-de-Bigorre in the French Pyrenees (Stallworthy, *Owen*, pp. 100–11; Stallworthy, pp. 275–6). He did not, in fact, reach Bagnères-de-Bigorre until 31 January 1914 and, so far as is known, was not then keeping a diary. The poem is an early example of his sustained use of 'pararhyme', Edmund Blunden's term for what has long been considered Owen's important prosodic innovation: the rhyming of words with a common consonantal outline but differing medial vowels (Leaves/Lives; Birds/Bards). Owen may have been aware of the earlier pararhyming of William Barnes's 'On the Road'.

19. *A maid*: Probably Nénette Léger, an eleven-year-old to whom he was giving private tuition.

Apologia pro Poemate Meo

Written in November–December 1917 at Scarborough, this may be a response to a remark made by Robert Graves in a letter to Owen, *c.* 22 December 1917: 'For God's sake cheer up and write more optimistically – the war's not ended yet but a poet should have a spirit above wars' (Owen and Bell, p. 596; Stallworthy, *Owen*, pp. 250–51, 252; Stallworthy, pp. 278–81).

Title: Sassoon corrected the flawed Latin of Owen's title, 'Apologia pro Poema Mea', which may have been prompted by that of Cardinal Newman's exposition of his spiritual history, *Apologia Pro Vita Sua*.

1. *I, too*: Perhaps an allusion to Robert Graves's poem, 'Two Fusiliers'.
13. *exultation*: Cf. Shelley, 'A Defence of Poetry': 'Poetry is a mirror which makes beautiful that which is distorted. [. . . I]t exalts the beauty of that which is most beautiful, and it adds beauty to that which is most deformed; it marries exultation and horror.'
19–20 *For love . . . eyes*: Cf. 'L'Amour', published in *The Nymph and Other Poems* (November 1917), by Owen's cousin, Leslie Gunston (lines 1–2): 'Love is the binding of souls together, / The binding of lips, the binding of eyes.'
21. *By Joy*: Cf. Keats, 'Ode on Melancholy' (line 22): 'And Joy, whose hand is ever at his lips'.

Le Christianisme

The MS of this poem, which was written in late November or early December 1917, probably at Scarborough, carries the name 'Quivières', a village where Owen was quartered in April 1917 (Stallworthy, *Owen*, p. 183; Stallworthy, p. 281). Quivières, however, has no church, so his memory may have been at fault. On 1 May, the battalion medical officer had found his recollections confused.

4. *our trouble*: Cf. Housman, 'On Wenlock Edge the wood's in trouble' (lines 19–20): 'Today the Roman and his trouble / Are ashes under Uricon'. See also 'Uriconium' (and note to line 15).
8. *a piece of hell*: 'Piece' meaning both 'fragment' and 'field-gun', as opposed to 'the peace of God'.

'Cramped in that funnelled hole'

Written probably on 4 December 1917 at Scarborough, this fragment was expertly reconstructed by Edmund Blunden (Stallworthy, *Owen*, pp. 245–6, 256, 257; Stallworthy, pp. 511–13).

1. *Cramped*: Cf. Henri Barbusse, *Under Fire* (1917): 'The soldier held his peace. In the distance he saw the night as *they* would pass it – cramped up, trembling with vigilance in the deep darkness, at the bottom of the listening-hole whose ragged jaws

showed in black outline all around whenever a gun hurled its dawn into the sky' (trans. W. Fitzwater Bray (1917); Everyman's Library, 1926), p. 126).

3–5 *death's jaws . . . Hell*: Cf. Tennyson, 'The Charge of the Light Brigade' (lines 24-5): 'Into the jaws of Death, / Into the mouth of Hell'. Like other of Owen's visions of the descent into hell such as 'Uriconium' and 'The Show', the 'hole' is described in terms of the human body.

Hospital Barge

Written in December 1917 at Scarborough, following 'a Saturday night revel in "Passing of Arthur"' (Blunden, p. 124; Stallworthy, *Owen*, pp. 248–9; Stallworthy, pp. 281–3). On 10 May 1917, Owen had written to his mother:

> I sailed in a steam-tug about 6 miles down the Canal with another 'inmate'. The heat of the afternoon was Augustan; and it has probably added another year to my old age to have been able to escape marching in equipment under such a sun. The scenery was such as I never saw or dreamed of since I read the *Fairie Queene*. Just as in the Winter when I woke up lying on the burning cold snow I fancied I must have died & been pitch-forked into the Wrong Place, so, yesterday, it was not more difficult to imagine that my dusky barge was wending up to Avalon, and the peace of Arthur, and where Lancelot heals him of his grievous wound. But the Saxon is not broken, as we could very well hear last night. Later, a real thunderstorm did its best to seem terrible, and quite failed.
>
> (Owen and Bell, p. 457)

2. *Cérisy*: A village a mile and a half down the Somme Canal from Gailly, where Owen was a patient in the 13th Casualty Clearing Station.

9. *One reading*: The poem suggests that its speaker may have been reading Malory, *Morte Darthur*, or a later retelling such as Tennyson, 'The Passing of Arthur', from *The Holy Grail and Other Poems* (1870), a copy of which Owen had bought in Edinburgh in July 1917.

12. *lamentation*: Cf. Tennyson, 'The Passing of Arthur' (lines 361–71):

> Then saw they how there hove a dusky barge,
> Dark as a funeral scarf from stem to stern,
> Beneath them; and descending they were ware

That all the decks were dense with stately forms,
Black-stoled, black-hooded, like a dream – by these
Three Queens with crowns of gold: and from them rose
A cry that shivered to the tingling stars,
And, as it were one voice, an agony
Of lamentation, like a wind that shrills
All night in a waste land, where no one comes,
Or hath come, since the making of the world.

14. *Merlin*: In November 1917 Owen had marked in his copy of Alfred Austin, *Songs of England* (1898), 'The Passing of Merlin' (v):

A wailing cometh from the shores that veil
Avilion's island valley; on the mere,
Looms through the mist and wet winds weeping blear
A dusky barge, which, without oar or sail,
Fades to the far-off fields where falls nor snow nor hail.

At a Calvary near the Ancre

Written, probably in late 1917 or early 1918 and a memory of fighting near the River Ancre in January 1917 (Stallworthy, p. 287), the only manuscript of this poem is in Susan Owen's autograph. Dominic Hibberd has skilfully unpacked a compact allegory:

As in 'The Parable of the Old Man and the Young', Owen adapts Biblical detail to fit the war. In the Gospel story, the *Soldiers* kept watch at the cross while Christ's *disciples* hid in fear of the authorities; *priests* and *scribes* passed by in scorn. The Church sends priests to the trenches, where they watch the common soldier being, as it were, crucified, and they take pride in minor wounds (*flesh-marked*, line 7) as a sign of their opposition to Germany (*the Beast*). *Flesh-marked*, however, carries a further meaning: the Devil used to be believed to leave his finger-marks on the flesh of his followers (cf. Revelation 14:9-10). Thus the Church's hatred of Germany (line 12) puts it in the Devil's following; and the priests' wounds are signs not so much of opposition to the Devil Germany as of allegiance to the Devil War. Christ said 'Love one another' *and* 'Love your enemies'; despite the exhortations of Church and State, Owen perceives that 'pure Christianity will not fit in with pure patriotism'.

(Owen and Bell, p. 461; Hibberd, p. 116)

Title: Calvary or Golgotha ('the place of the skull', from the Latin *calvaria* and the Hebrew *gulgõleth*) was the site of the Crucifixion. A Calvary is a model of Christ on the Cross, commonly found at French country crossroads. (See Gurney, 'Crucifix Corner', and note on its title.)

4. *bear with*: Two senses seem intended: 'humour' and 'carry the cross with'.

11–12 *greater love . . . life*: Cf. John 15:13: 'Greater love hath no man than this, that a man lay down his life for his friends.' See also 'Greater Love', drafted at much the same time.

Miners

Written on 13 or 14 January 1918 at Scarborough (Stallworthy, *Owen*, pp. 253–5, 256–7; Stallworthy, p. 287), this is Owen's response to newspaper accounts of a pit explosion at Podmore Hall Colliery, the previous day, resulting in the deaths of about 140 men and boy miners. On 14 January, he wrote to his mother: 'Wrote a poem on the Colliery Disaster: but I get mixed up with the War at the end. It is short, but oh! sour' (Blunden, p. 125). He showed the poem to Sassoon, who proposed alterations which, with questionable judgement, Owen would seem to have accepted (as they appear in the text he sent to the *Nation*). On 17 January, Owen sent his mother 'the Coal Poem' and two days later wrote to her: 'With your beautiful letter came a proof from the *Nation* of my "Miners". This is the first poem I have sent to the *Nation* myself, and it has evidently been accepted. It was scrawled out on the back of a note to the Editor; and no penny stamp or addressed envelope was enclosed for return! That's the way to do it. "Miners" will probably appear next Saturday [26 January]' (Owen and Bell, pp. 527–8). It did.

In 'Miners', the watcher by the hearth expects the coal to tell of its prehistoric origin – Owen was an amateur geologist – but instead it speaks of the sufferings of miners, in whom Owen had been interested (Stallworthy, *Owen*, pp. 76–8, 136–7, 230) long before he commanded a platoon containing several miners in 1916. The Halmerend disaster prompts a vision of the fate of such men and those others who dug perilous 'saps' under No Man's Land to mine the enemy lines. At the poem's end Owen sees himself sharing their common trench, mine, grave, hell. His control of the prosodic innovation, pararhyme, is nowhere more sophisticated and successful; the vowel-pitch rising (loads/lids) with delight, falling (lads) with despair.

8. *fauns*: Owen wrote 'fawns'.
19. *Many . . . charred*: The *Nation* printed Sassoon's suggestion, '(For many hearts with coal are charred)', written above Owen's uncancelled line on the surviving MS; and, in 34, Sassoon's suggestion, 'Lost', written beneath Owen's uncancelled 'Left'.

The Letter

Written between January and March 1918, probably at Scarborough but possibly at Ripon (Stallworthy, p. 288), this develops the use of direct speech – learnt from Sassoon – that Owen had first attempted in 'Inspection'.

1. *B.E.F.*: British Expeditionary Force.
5. *'Uns*: Huns.
14. *out in rest*: Out of the Front Line in a rest area.
16. *sov*: Sovereign, British gold coin nominally worth £1.
18. *Stand to*: See Gurney, 'Laventie', note to line 35.
21. *iodine*: Brand of disinfectant.

Conscious

Written between January and March 1918, probably at Scarborough but possibly at Ripon (Stallworthy, pp. 288–9), this shows the influence of Sassoon's poem 'The Death Bed'.

3. *yellow mayflowers:* On 8 May 1917, Owen wrote to his sister from 13th Casualty Clearing Station: 'Meanwhile I have superb weather, sociable-possible friends, great blue bowls of yellow Mayflower, baths and bed *ad lib*' (Owen and Bell, p. 456).
9. *sudden evening*: On 14 August 1912, he wrote to his mother: 'sudden twilight seemed to fall upon the world' (Owen and Bell, p. 153).
10. *water*: Cf. Sassoon, 'The Death Bed' (line 7): 'Someone was holding water to his mouth.'
12. *crimson slaughter*: Cf. Sassoon, 'The Death Bed' (line 9): 'Through crimson gloom to darkness'.

Dulce et Decorum Est

Drafted in the first half of October 1917 at Craiglockhart, this poem was revised between January and March 1918 probably at Scarborough but possibly at Ripon (Stallworthy, *Owen*, pp. 226–8; Stallworthy, pp. 292–7). The earliest surviving MS is dated 'Oct. 8, 1917', and on the 16th [?] Owen wrote to his mother: 'Here is a gas poem, done yesterday, (which is not private, but not final). The famous Latin tag [from Horace, *Odes*, III.ii.13] means of course It is sweet and meet to die for one's country. Sweet! and decorous!' (Owen and Bell, pp. 499–500). Like many others, Owen had earlier taken a different view: his unpublished poem of 1914, 'The Ballad of Purchase-Money', asserting:

O meet it is and passing sweet
To live in peace with others,
But sweeter still and far more meet
To die in war for brothers.
(Stallworthy, p. 507)

5. *Men . . . Many*: On 16 January 1917, Owen wrote to his mother of 'craters full of water. Men have been known to drown in them. Many stuck in the mud' (Owen and Bell, p. 427).
8. *Five-nines*: 5.9-calibre shells.
9. *GAS*: On 19 January 1917, he wrote to her: 'I went on ahead to scout – foolishly alone – and when, half a mile away from the party, got overtaken by GAS' (Owen and Bell, p. 428).
12. *flound'ring*: Harold Owen remembered his brother 'using this word floundering and, unable to resist the play, adding, "[. . .] but of course there is, I suppose, the possibility you might founder"' (H. Owen, III, 132).
13. *panes*: The gas mask's celluloid windows.
25. *My friend*: Jessie Pope, to whom the poem (its MSS show) was originally to have been dedicated, was the author of many pre-war children's books as well as of *Jessie Pope's War Poems* (1915), *More War Poems* (1915) and *Simple Rhymes for Stirring Times* (1916) (Stallworthy, *Owen*, p. 227).

Insensibility

Drafted either in October–November 1917 at Craiglockhart, or between November 1917 and January 1918 at Scarborough, this Pindaric ode may be a response to Wordsworth's 'Character of the Happy Warrior' (Stallworthy, *Owen*, p. 261; Stallworthy, pp. 301–6). It may have been revised at Ripon in April 1918. Owen wrote to his cousin Leslie Gunston on the 21st of that month: 'In my Chaumbers under the roof of a cottage (7 Borrage Lane, Ripon) I have written,

I think, two poems: one an Ode which, considering my tuneless tendencies, may be called dam good, excuse me' (Owen and Bell, pp. 546–7). Dominic Hibberd, however, has argued (in a letter to the editors) that Owen is referring to his 'Elegy in April and September' which, in its April version, was entitled 'Ode for a Poet' (Stallworthy, pp. 184 and 362).

Title: Cf. Shelley, 'A Defence of Poetry':

> [Poetry] is as it were the interpenetration of a diviner nature through our own; but its footsteps are like those of a wind over a sea, which the coming calm erases, and those traces remain only, as on the wrinkled sand which paves it. These and corresponding conditions of being are experienced principally by those of the most delicate sensibility and the most enlarged imagination; and the state of mind produced by them is at war with every base desire.

1. *Happy are men*: Cf. Wordsworth, 'Character of the Happy Warrior' (lines 1–2): 'Who is the happy Warrior? Who is he / That every man in arms should wish to be?'

5. *cobbled with their brothers*: On 25 [?] March 1918, Owen wrote to his mother: 'They are dying again at Beaumont Hamel, which already in 1916 was cobbled with skulls' (Owen and Bell, p. 542).

8. *fooling*: Cf. Owen, 'Six O'clock in Princes Street' (line 5): 'Neither should I go fooling over clouds' (Stallworthy, pp. 102 and 255–6).

9. *gaps for filling*: 'Fill up the ranks!' was a familiar wartime recruiting slogan.

17. *shilling*: The 'King's shilling' was that traditionally given to a newly enlisted soldier by the recruiting officer.

19. *Happy*: Owen repeats this word throughout the poem to distinguish soldiers, whose sensibilities (see note to Title) have been dulled by battle, from 'We wise' (line 40), soldier-poets of 'delicate sensibility' and 'enlarged imagination'.

28–9 *scorching cautery . . . ironed*: Bleeding veins can be staunched, cauterized, with red-hot iron.

56. *the last sea and the hapless stars*: Cf. Tennyson, 'Oenone' (line 215): 'Between the loud stream and the trembling stars'.

59. *reciprocity*: Cf. John Drinkwater, 'Reciprocity', a poem printed in the Craiglockhart Hospital magazine, *The Hydra*, new series, no. 1, 2. There is a MS of the poem among Owen's papers.

Strange Meeting

Drafted between January and March 1918, probably at Scarborough but possibly at Ripon, this poem incorporates and develops earlier fragments (*WO*, 215, 256-7; Stallworthy, pp. 306–10). For a full and illuminating discussion of the interplay of echoes in 'Strange Meeting' from the sources below and Sir Lewis Morris, see Bäckman, pp. 96–117. The MSS suggest that Owen may not have regarded the poem as complete.

Title: Cf. Shelley, *The Revolt of Islam* (lines 1828–32):

> And one whose spear had pierced me, leaned beside,
> With quivering lips and humid eyes; – and all
> Seemed like some brothers on a journey wide
> Gone forth, whom now strange meeting did befall
> In a strange land [. . .]

Cf. also Harold Monro, *Strange Meetings* (1917).

2. *tunnel*: Cf. Sassoon, 'The Rear Guard' (lines 1–3): 'Groping along the tunnel, step by step, / He winked his prying torch with patching glare / From side to side, and sniffed the unwholesome air.' Bäckman suggests the influence of a childhood memory of a nightmare walk down an 'immensely long and dark' drive, roofed with trees 'so that the effect was of a rather dark tunnel' (H. Owen, I, 80).

2. *scooped*: Cf. Shelley, *The Revolt of Islam* (lines 2913–15):

> He plunged through the green silence of the main,
> Through many a cavern which the eternal flood
> Had scooped, as dark lairs for its monster brood [. . .]

Also *Alastor* (lines 423–5):

> There, huge caves,
> Scooped in the dark of their aëry rocks
> Mocking its moans, respond and roar for ever.

3. *granites*: On 18 [?] February 1917, Owen wrote to his mother: 'the men had to dig trenches in ground like granite' (Owen and Bell, p. 436).

4. *encumbered*: On 1 February 1916, he wrote to her: 'When I was going up the subway at Liverpool St. from the Underground to

the Gt. Eastern Platform, I noticed the passages unduly encumbered, and found the outlet just closed' (Owen and Bell, p. 377).

6–11 *Then . . . grained*: Cf. the poet's vision of Moneta's face, 'bright-blanched / By an immortal sickness which kills not' in Keats, 'The Fall of Hyperion'; also Dante, *Hell* (in the 1805 translation by the Revd Henry Francis Cary, a copy of which Owen possessed), XV, 22–9:

> I was agnized of one, who by the skirt
> Caught me, and cried, 'What wonder have we here?'
> And I, when he to me outstretch'd his arm,
> Intently fix'd my ken on his parch'd looks,
> That, although smirch'd with fire, they hinder'd not
> But I remember'd him; and towards his face
> My hand inclining, answer'd, 'Sir Brunetto!
> And are ye here?'

25. *The pity of war*: Cf. his draft Preface.

28. *They will be swift*: Cf. 2 Samuel 1:23: 'Saul and Jonathan were lovely and pleasant in their lives, and in their death they were not divided: they were swifter than eagles, they were stronger than lions.'

29. *trek*: Presumably an allusion to the Great Trek of the South African Boer farmers in 1835–6.

32. *miss the march*: Cf. Owen's 'The Fates', 14: 'And miss the march of lifetime, stage by stage' (Stallworthy, p. 87).

34. *chariot-wheels*: Cf. Shelley, *Queen Mab*, VII, 33–5: 'whether hosts / Stain his death-blushing chariot-wheels, as on / Triumphantly they roll'.

36. *truths that lie too deep*: Cf. Wordsworth's ode on 'Intimations of Immortality from Recollections of Early Childhood' (line 205): 'Thoughts that do often lie too deep for tears'.

39. *Foreheads . . . have bled*: Cf. Luke 22:44: 'and his sweat was as it were great drops of blood falling down to the ground'.

40. *I am the enemy . . . my friend*: Cf. Oscar Wilde, 'The Ballad of Reading Gaol' (line 37): 'Yet each man kills the thing he loves.' This line, misquoted, appears in a fragment drafted by Owen in late 1917 (Stallworthy, p. 492). Cf. also Henri Barbusse, *Under Fire* (1917) (p. 288): 'When I'm sleeping I dream I'm killing him over again!'

44. *Let us sleep now*: Cf. the cancelled line in Owen's unfinished poem, 'The Women & the Slain', drafted in 1914: 'Keep silent. Let us sleep' (Stallworthy, p. 502).

Asleep

Drafted on 14 November 1917 probably in Shrewsbury, and revised the following May at Ripon (Stallworthy, *Owen*, pp. 237–238; Stallworthy, pp. 312–14). On 16 November 1917, Owen wrote to Leslie Gunston: 'Good of you to send me the Lyric of Nov. 14th. I can only send my own of the same date, which came from Winchester Downs, as I crossed the long backs of the downs after leaving you. It is written as from the trenches. I could almost see the dead lying about in the hollows of the downs' (Owen and Bell, p. 508). The subject of the poem suggests a knowledge of Rimbaud's 'Le dormeur du val'. Dominic Hibberd argues persuasively for the influence of Robert Graves's *Fairies and Fusiliers* (1917), which Owen bought on the day he began 'Asleep' ('Wilfred Owen and the Georgians', *RES*, n.s., 30:117 (1979), 36); and Bäckman detects and discusses (40–42) an important debt to Milton's 'Lycidas'.

1–9 *Under . . . track*: Cf. Swinburne, 'Laus Veneris' (lines 1–4):

> Asleep or waking is it? For her neck,
> Kissed over close, wears yet a purple speck
> Wherein the painted blood falters and goes out;
> Soft, and stung softly – fairer for a fleck.

17. *hair . . . grey grass*: On 24 May 1914, Owen wrote to his mother: 'It was curious you asked about my grey hairs, for just last week I noticed they were cropping up again. In winter they died down, with the grass' (Owen and Bell, p. 252).

Arms and the Boy

Written, or at any rate fair-copied on 3 May 1918 at 7 Borrage Lane, Ripon, this poem was classified by Owen in his draft list of contents under 'Protest – the unnaturalness of weapons' (Stallworthy, pp. 315 and 359).

Title: Cf. Sassoon, 'Arms and the Man', and Harold Monro, 'Youth in Arms'.

1–4 *Let . . . flesh*: Cf. Shelley, *The Mask of Anarchy* (lxxvii, lines 311–14):

> Let the fixèd bayonet
> Gleam with sharp desire to wet
> Its bright point in English blood
> Looking keen as one for food.

6. *nuzzle*: Paul Fussell notes that 'Bret Harte's "What the Bullet Sang", one of the few American poems available in the *Oxford Book* [*of English Verse*, ed. Sir Arthur Quiller-Couch], seems to lie behind both Sassoon's "The Kiss" and Owen's "Arms and the Boy", both of which, like [Bret] Harte's poem, make much of the quasi-erotic desire of the bullet (and in Sassoon, the bayonet) to "kiss" or "nuzzle" the body of its adolescent target' (*The Great War and Modern Memory*, p. 160).

The Show

Drafted in November 1917 at Scarborough and revised in May 1918 at Ripon (Stallworthy, *Owen*, pp. 243–4, 245; Stallworthy, pp. 316–17), this is almost certainly the poem referred to in Owen's letter of 27 November 1917: 'My "Vision" is the result of two hours' leisure yesterday, – and getting up early this morning! If you have objections to make, would you return it? If not, pass it on to R[obbie]. R[oss]' (Owen and Bell, p. 512). That this 'Vision' was what came to be 'The Show' (and not the fragmentary 'A Vision in Whitechapel', later retitled 'Lines to a Beauty seen in Limehouse' (Stallworthy, pp. 481–2), as Owen and Bell suggest) is made clear by Owen's letter of 6 December 1917: 'What do you think of my Vowel-rime stunt in this ['Wild with all Regrets', to become 'A Terre'], and "Vision"?' (Owen and Bell, p. 514).

Owen's vision derives from his experience of battlefields between January and May 1917 and from his reading in November–December 1917 of Henri Barbusse, *Under Fire* (1917). From Chapter i, 'The Vision':

> *The man at the end of the rank cries, 'I can see crawling things down there' – 'Yes, as though they were alive' – 'Some sort of plant perhaps' – 'Some kind of men' –*
>
> *And there amid the baleful glimmers of the storm, below the dark disorder of the clouds that extend and unfurl over the earth like evil spirits, they seem to see a great livid plain unrolled, which to their seeing is made of mud and water, while figures appear and fast fix themselves to the surface of it, all blinded and borne down with filth, like the dreadful castaways of shipwreck. And it seems to them that these are soldiers.* (p. 4)

'The Show' may also echo two passages from chapter xx: 'Dwarfed to the size of insects and worms, they make a queer dark stirring among these shadow-hidden and Death-pacified lands' (p. 255); and 'In the middle of the plateau and in the depth of the rainy and bitter air, on the ghastly morrow of this debauch of slaughter, there is a head planted in the ground, a wet and bloodless head, with a heavy beard. It is one of ours, and the helmet is beside it' (p. 265; see also line 29 and note).

Title: 'Show' was soldiers' slang for 'battle'. Cf. 'The Chances', line 1.
Epigraph: Owen misquotes Forgael's speech in Yeats's play *The Shadowy Waters* (*Poems 1899–1905* (1906), p. 22), which reads: 'burnished mirror' (Stallworthy, *Owen*, p. 245).

4–5 *cratered ... plagues*: Owen wrote to his mother on 19 January 1917: '[No Man's Land] is pock-marked like a body of foulest disease and its odour is the breath of cancer. [...] No Man's Land under snow is like the face of the moon chaotic, crater-ridden, uninhabitable, awful, the abode of madness' (Owen and Bell, p. 429).

17. *Brown ... spines*: The caterpillars 'with bristling spines' are files of soldiers: the Germans in grey uniforms, the British in khaki.

26–7 *And ... further*: On 14 May 1917, Owen wrote to his brother Colin: 'Then we were caught in a Tornado of Shells. The various "waves" were all broken up and we carried on like a crowd moving off a cricket-field. When I looked back and saw the ground all crawling and wormy with wounded bodies, I felt no horror at all but only an immense exultation at having got through the Barrage' (Owen and Bell, p. 458).

29. *fresh-severed head*: See headnote. As the commander of a platoon advancing in single file, Owen would have been literally and figuratively its 'head'.

Futility

Written in May 1918 at Ripon and published in the *Nation* (15 June 1918), this poem shows the influence of Tennyson's elegy *In Memoriam* (Stallworthy, pp. 319–21).

Title: Cf. Tennyson, *In Memoriam* (lvi, line 25): 'O life as futile, then, as frail!'

7. *old sun*: Cf. Donne, 'The Sun Rising' (line 1): 'Busy old fool, unruly sun'.

8–9 *it wakes ... cold star*: Cf. John Davidson, 'Thirty Bob a Week' (lines 71-2): 'A little sleeping seed, I woke – I did, indeed – / A million years before the blooming sun.' Also Sir Walter Scott, Hymn 487, *The English Hymnal* (lines 9–12): 'O, on that day, that wrathful day, / When man to judgement wakes from clay, / Be thou the trembling sinner's stay, / Though heaven and earth shall pass away!'

The End

Begun probably in late 1916; continued either in October–November 1917 at Craiglockhart, or between November 1917 and January 1918 at Scarborough (Stallworthy, pp. 322–6); this poem is almost certainly the one referred to in Owen's letter of 12 February 1917 to his mother: 'Leslie [Gunston] tells me that Miss Joergens considers my Sonnet on "The End" the finest of the lot. Naturally, because it is, intentionally, in her style!' (Owen and Bell, p. 434). 'To Eros' (Stallworthy, p. 115) was also, at one time, entitled 'The End', as was an unfinished fragment (ibid., p. 491). A poem of Gunston's, 'The End', was published in *YM / The British Empire YMCA Weekly*, ii:102 (22 December 1916), 1229.

6. *all tears assuage*: Cf. Revelation 21:4: 'And God shall wipe away all tears from their eyes; and there shall be no more death, neither sorrow, nor crying.' For Susan Owen's misleading quotation of lines 5–6 on her son's tombstone, see Stallworthy, *Owen*, p. 288.
14. *titanic tears*: Cf. 'Strange Meeting', line 3.

S.I.W.

Drafted in September 1917 at Craiglockhart and revised in May 1918 at Ripon, this poem shows the influence of Sassoon's poems such as 'The Hero' and 'Stand-to: Good Friday Morning' (Stallworthy, pp. 327–31).

Title: Military abbreviation for 'Self-Inflicted Wound'.
Epigraph: From Yeats's play, *The King's Threshold (Poems 1899–1905* (1906), p. 238).

10. *Y. M. Hut*: Young Men's Christian Association hostel.
28. *ball*: Technical military term for 'bullet'.
31. *blind trench*: One with no outlet.
32. *creeping fire*: A 'creeping barrage' advanced a predetermined distance – usually in front of advancing infantry – at a predetermined time.

The Next War

Written in late September 1917 at Craiglockhart, Owen sent this sonnet, with 'Anthem for Doomed Youth', to his mother on the 25th (Owen and Bell, p. 496). On 2 October 1917, he wrote to her: 'I included my "Next War" in order to strike a note. I want Colin to read, mark, learn etc. it' (ibid., p. 497). The poem was revised in

July 1918 at Scarborough (Stallworthy, *Owen*, p. 216; Stallworthy, pp. 334–6).

Epigraph: 'A Letter Home' (to Robert Graves, written at Flixécourt in May 1916, lines 73–4).

14. *on*: Against.

Greater Love

Drafted either in October–November 1917 at Craiglockhart or between November 1917 and January 1918 at Scarborough, and revised that July at Scarborough (Stallworthy, *Owen*, pp. 230–31; Stallworthy, pp. 337–41), this poem is a response to Swinburne's 'Before the Mirror / (Verses Written under a Picture) / Inscribed to J.A. Whistler' (lines 1–7):

> White rose in red rose-garden
> Is not so white;
> Snowdrops that plead for pardon
> And pine for fright
> Because the hard East blows
> Over their maiden rows
>
> Grow not as this face grows from pale to bright.

Owen may also have been aware of Salomé's words to Jokanaan in Wilde's *Salomé*: 'The roses in the garden of the Queen of Arabia are not so white as thy body.' He wrote to his mother on 16 [?] May 1917: 'Christ is literally in no man's land. There men often hear His voice: Greater love hath no man than this, that a man lay down his life – for a friend' (Owen and Bell, p. 461).

Title: Cf. John 15:13: 'Greater love hath no man than this, that a man lay down his life for his friends.' See also 'At a Calvary Near the Ancre', lines 11–12.

20. *hearts made great*: Cf. Elizabeth Barrett Browning, *Aurora Leigh*, Second Book (lines 718–20): 'As my blood recoiled / From that imputed ignominy, I made / My heart great with it.' See also Owen's letter of 2 April 1916 to his mother: 'And the drums pulse fearfully-voluptuously, as great hearts in death' (Owen and Bell, p. 388).
21. *pale*: Cf. headnote.
22. *trail*: Used in the military sense of 'trail arms', carry a rifle with butt end near the ground and muzzle pointing forwards.
24. *touch them not*: Cf. John 20:15–17: 'Jesus saith unto [Mary

Magdalene], Woman, why weepest thou? [. . .] Jesus saith unto her, Touch me not; for I am not yet ascended to my Father.'

The Last Laugh

Drafted in February 1918 at Scarborough, an early version of this poem was included in Owen's letter of 18 February to his mother, and was there prefaced: 'There is a point where prayer is indistinguishable from blasphemy. There is also a point where blasphemy is indistinguishable from prayer. As in the first verse [. . .]' (Owen and Bell, p. 534). The first of the three later drafts, in which full rhymes have given place to pararhymes, is dated '5.3.18', and Owen's subsequent revisions must date from spring–summer 1918 when he gave a final fair copy to Osbert Sitwell (Stallworthy, *Owen*, p. 258; Stallworthy, p. 341).

Mental Cases

Drafted in May 1918 at Ripon and revised in July at Scarborough, this poem draws on the earlier, fragmentary, 'Purgatorial Passions' (Stallworthy, pp. 455–6). Owen wrote to his mother on 25 May 1918: 'I've been "busy" this evening with my terrific poem (at present) called "The Deranged". This poem the Editor of the *Burlington Magazine* – (a 2/6 Arts Journal which takes no poetry) – old More Adey, I say, solemnly prohibited me from sending to the *English Review*, on the grounds that "the *English Review* should not be encouraged"!!!' (Owen and Bell, p. 553). On 15 June he told his mother: 'lo! An urgent request from the Sitwells in London for more of my poems for their 1918 Anthology which is coming out immediately. This is on the strength of "The Deranged", which S. Moncrieff showed them the other day' (ibid., p. 559). In the event, the Sitwells printed none of Owen's poems in *Wheels* (1918).

The poem reflects Owen's reading of Dante, and Mark Sinfield points out that the opening of each stanza echoes the diction and, with bitter irony, parallels the structure of Revelation 7:13–17 (*Notes & Queries* (August 1982), 339–41).

12. *Multitudinous murders*: Cf. *Macbeth*, II, ii, 58-60: 'No; this my hand will rather / The multitudinous seas incarnadine, / Making the green one red.'

26. *rope-knouts of their scourging*: Cf. Owen's 'The Rime of the Youthful Mariner' (lines 1–4; Stallworthy, p. 131):

One knotted a rope with an evil knout,
  And flogged me till I fell;
And he is picking the rope end out
  In a land-locked prison-cell.

The Chances

Drafted in August–September 1917 at Craiglockhart, this poem shows the strong influence of Sassoon's 'The Bishop'. It was revised in July 1918 at Scarborough (Stallworthy, pp. 345–6).

1. *show*: Soldiers' slang for 'battle'.
5. *cushy*: Soldiers' slang for 'slightly'.
6. *Scuppered ... nowt*: Soldiers' (from nautical) slang for 'killed' and dialect for 'nothing', respectively.
8. *props*: Soldiers' slang for 'legs'.
10. *Fritz*: Soldiers' slang for 'the Germans'.
12. *blighty*: See Gurney, 'Ballad of the Three Spectres', note to line 8.

The Send-Off

Drafted in April–May 1918 at Ripon and revised in July at Scarborough (Stallworthy, *Owen*, pp. 261–2; Stallworthy, pp. 346–50), this may be one of the 'two poems' mentioned in Owen's letter to Leslie Gunston of 21 April 1918 (Owen and Bell, p. 547). On 4 May he was able to tell his mother: 'I have long "waited" for a final stanza to "the Draft" (which begins.

I

"Down the deep, darkening lanes they sang their way
To the waiting train,
And filled its doors with faces grimly gay,
And heads & shoulders white with wreath & spray,
As men's are, slain.")'

(Owen and Bell, p. 550)

6–8 *Dull porters ... camp*: Bäckman writes: 'These lines contain a couple of ironic echoes of stanzas 25 and 27 of Gray's "Elegy", where a "hoary-headed swain" is heard to say that he had often seen the departed country poet "brushing with hasty steps the dews away, / To meet the sun upon *the upland lawn*", but then suddenly "one morn", he "*miss'd* him on the custom'd hill"' (p. 43).

The Parable of the Old Man and the Young

Written in July 1918, probably at Scarborough, lines 1–14 follow the wording of Genesis 22:1–19 very closely (Stallworthy, pp. 350–51).

7. *belts and straps*: As of a soldier's equipment.
16. *seed*: Cf. '1914', line 14.

Disabled

Drafted in October 1917 at Craiglockhart, this was revised in July 1918 at Scarborough (Stallworthy, *Owen*, pp. 224–6; Stallworthy, pp. 351–3). On 14 October 1917, Owen wrote to his mother: 'On Sat. I met Robert Graves [. . .] No doubt he thought me a slacker sort of sub. S.S. when they were together showed him my longish war-piece "Disabled" (you haven't seen it) & it seems Graves was mightily impressed, and considers me a kind of Find!! No thanks, Captain Graves! I'll find myself in due time' (Owen and Bell, p. 499). On 18 October he told her that Graves had 'carried away a Poem, or was carried away with it, without my knowledge. It was only in a Draft State, & I was perfectly aware of all the solecisms' (ibid., p. 501). A day or two earlier, Graves had written to Owen about that 'damn fine poem of yours, that "Disabled"' (ibid., p. 595).

22. *carried shoulder-high*: Cf. Housman, 'To an Athlete Dying Young', lines 1–4:

> The time you won your town the race
> We chaired you through the market-place;
> Man and boy stood cheering by,
> And home we brought you shoulder-high.

23. *peg*: Slang expression for a drink, usually brandy and soda.
25. *kilts*: And 'daggers in plaid socks' (line 33) are worn by soldiers in Scottish regiments.
27. *jilts*: Capricious women.
29. *they wrote his lie*: The recruiting officers entered on his enlistment form his lie that he was nineteen years old and therefore above the minimum age for military service.
45. *Why don't they come*: See Rosenberg, 'Dead Man's Dump', line 71 and note.

A Terre

Begun in December 1917 at Scarborough, this was revised in April 1918 at Ripon and again in July at Scarborough (Stallworthy, pp. 354–6). On 3 December 1917, Owen wrote to his mother: 'I finished an important poem this afternoon' (Owen and Bell, p. 513), and three days later to Sassoon: 'This "Wild with all Regrets" was begun & ended two days ago, at one gasp. If simplicity, if imaginativeness, if sympathy, if resonance of vowels, make poetry I have not succeeded. But if you say "Here is poetry," it will be so for me. What do you think of my Vowel-rime stunt in this, and "Vision"? Do you consider the hop from Flea to Soul too abrupt?' (ibid., p. 514).

Title: 'To Earth' (French). Cf. 'The Order for the Burial of the Dead': 'earth to earth, ashes to ashes'. Owen changed the title in his April 1918 revision.

5. *peg out*: Slang expression for die.
7. *pennies*: It was once customary to place coins on the eyelids of a corpse to keep them closed.
13. *puffy, bald*: Cf. Sassoon, 'Base Details' (lines 1–4):

> If I were fierce, and bald, and short of breath,
> I'd live with scarlet Majors at the Base,
> And speed glum heroes up the line to death.
> You'd see me with my puffy petulant face [. . .]

19. *fifty years ahead*: Cf. Housman, 'Loveliest of trees, the cherry now' (lines 9–12):

> And since to look at things in bloom
> Fifty springs are little room,
> About the woodlands I will go
> To see the cherry hung with snow.

30. *dirt*: Cf. 'Inspection', line 8.
34. *sweep*: Chimney-sweep.
36. *O Life . . . rat*: Cf. *King Lear*, V, iii, 307–8: 'Why should a dog, a horse, a rat, have life, / 'And thou no breath at all?'
44. *'I shall be one . . . stone'*: Cf. Shelley, 'Adonais' (xlii):

> He is made one with Nature: there is heard
> His voice in all her music, from the moan
> Of thunder, to the song of night's sweet bird;

He is a presence to be felt and known
In darkness and in light, from herb and stone,
Spreading itself where'er that Power may move
Which has withdrawn his being to its own [. . .]

47. *'Pushing up daisies'*: A common slang expression, meaning dead.
48–50 *my fat . . . man-soup:* Cf. Sassoon, 'The Tombstone-Maker' (lines 11–12): 'I told him with a sympathetic grin, / That Germans boil dead soldiers down for fat.'
55. *touch once*: Cf. 'Futility', lines 1–2.
60. *turned to fronds*: Cf. 'Miners', line 7.

The Kind Ghosts

Revised – it may have been written earlier – on 30 July 1918 at Scarborough, according to the dated MS (Stallworthy, p. 357), this may be the poem referred to in Owen's letter to his mother of 8 August 1918 (Owen and Bell, p. 567).

1. *She*: Probably Britannia. Dominic Hibberd notes that 'The word "Brittannia" (Owen's spelling was erratic) appears unexplained in a rough list of titles which he jotted down that summer; it seems likely to have been a draft title for this poem. Compare Swinburne's "Perinde ac Cadaver". While he was in France he acquired a copy of Swinburne's *Poems and Ballads*; it was probably the last book he read' (*Wilfred Owen* (Writers and Their Work, 1975), p. 35).
11. *hecatombs*: '[G]reat public sacrifices' (*OED*). Owen may have meant places of great public sacrifice. Alternatively, he may have used the word, incorrectly, to mean 'tombs' or confused it with 'catacombs'.

Exposure

Begun in December 1917 at Scarborough, when one unfinished line was written at the top of the MS of 'Cramped in that funnelled hole', this poem was revised there in early 1918, and in September 1918 finished in France (Stallworthy, *Owen*, pp. 246-8; Stallworthy, pp. 365-70). Owen appears to have dated the poem's final draft 'Feb. 1916', but the '6' could be an imperfect '8'. 'Exposure' was prompted by experiences he had described in a letter to his mother dated 4 February 1917 (Owen and Bell, pp. 430-32). On 22 April 1918, he wrote to her: 'to quote myself cynically "Nothing happens"' (ibid., p. 548), which suggests that 'Exposure' was far enough advanced for her to be expected to recognize its refrain. It appears, under the title 'Nothing happens', in one of the lists of contents drawn up at Ripon between March and June 1918 (Stallworthy, p. 539).

1. *Our brains ache*: An ironic echo of Keats, 'Ode to a Nightingale' (lines 1–2): 'My heart aches, and a drowsy numbness pains / My sense.'
3. *salient*: The front line in places jutted into enemy territory, and at such 'salients' the fighting tended to be fiercest.
9. *rumour of some other war*: Cf. Matthew 24:6: 'wars and rumours of wars'. Owen had written to Leslie Gunston on 25 July 1915: 'You say you "hear of wars and rumours of wars". *Vous en êtes là seulement*? You hear Rumours? The rumours, over here, make the ears of the gunners bleed' (Owen and Bell, p. 349).
14. *grey*: The German troops wore grey uniforms and, like the dawn, came from the east.
22. *We cringe in holes*: Cf. 'Cramped in that funnelled hole', line 1.
23. *drowse*: See note on line 1 above.
26. *home . . . glozed*: Cf. the song: 'Keep the home fires burning . . . Though your lads are far away they dream of home.' *glozed*: A conflation of 'glowing' and 'glazed'.
33. *God's invincible spring*: Cf. Owen, 'The Wrestlers' (Stallworthy, pp. 520–25, line 34): 'And all the ardour of the invincible spring'.
39. *All their eyes are ice*: Cf. Yeats, 'The Happy Townland' (line 11): 'Queens, their eyes blue like the ice'.

The Sentry

Begun between August and October 1917 at Craiglockhart, continued in May 1918 at Scarborough, and completed that September in France (Stallworthy, pp. 371–6), this must be one of the 'few poems' that accompanied Owen's letter of 22 September 1918 to Sassoon (Owen and Bell, p. 578). A year and a half before, on 16 January 1917, he had written to his mother: 'In the Platoon on my left the sentries over the dug-out were blown to nothing. One of these poor fellows was my first servant whom I rejected. If I had kept him he would have lived, for servants don't do Sentry Duty. I kept my own sentries half way down the stairs during the more terrific bombardment. In spite of this one lad was blown down and, I am afraid, blinded' (ibid., p. 428).

8. *whizz-bangs*: Small shells of such high velocity that the sound

made in passing through the air is almost simultaneous with the explosion.

22. *Eyeballs*: Cf. with the other tormented eyes that stare from 'Dulce et Decorum Est', line 19, and 'Greater Love', line 6.

25. *flound'ring*: Cf. letter of 16 January 1917 quoted in headnote: 'I was mercifully helped to do my duty and crawl, wade, climb and flounder over No Man's Land to visit my other post' (Owen and Bell, pp. 427–8).

28. *one . . . drowned himself*: Cf. letter quoted above: 'I nearly broke down and let myself drown in the water that was now slowly rising over my knees' (ibid., p. 427).

Smile, Smile, Smile

Written in mid to late September 1918 in France (Stallworthy, pp. 374–6). On the 22nd, Owen wrote to Sassoon:

> Did you see what the Minister of Labour said in the *Mail* the other day? 'The first instincts of the men after the cessation of hostilities will be to return home.' And again –
>
> 'All classes acknowledge their indebtedness to the soldiers & sailors . . . '
>
> About the same day, Clemenceau is reported by the *Times* as saying: 'All are worthy . . . yet we should be untrue to ourselves if we forgot that the greatest glory will be to the splendid poilus, who, etc'
>
> I began a Postscript to these Confessions, but hope you will already have lashed yourself, (lashed yourself!) into something . . .
>
> (Owen and Bell, p. 578)

The Times of 19 September 1918 had reported the French premier as saying:

> All are worthy of victory, because they will know how to honour it. Yet, however, in the ancient spot where sit the fathers of the Republic we should be untrue to ourselves if we forgot that the greatest glory will be to those splendid *poilus* [French slang for 'common soldiers'] who will see confirmed by history the titles of nobility which they themselves have earned. At the present moment they ask for nothing more than to be allowed to complete the great work which will assure them of immortality. What do they want and what do you? To keep on fighting victoriously until the moment when the enemy will understand there is no possible negotiation between crime and right.

Title: Taken from one of the most popular British songs on the Western Front, which begins:

What's the use of worrying?
It never was worth while,
So, pack up your troubles in your old kit-bag
And smile, smile, smile.

Spring Offensive

Begun in July 1918 probably at Scarborough, Owen's last poem was revised in mid to late September in France (Stallworthy, *Owen*, pp. 274–6; Stallworthy, pp. 376–9). He sent a fair copy of lines 1–17 with his letter of 22 September 1918 to Sassoon. An accompanying note asked: 'Is this worth going on with? I don't want to write anything to which a soldier would say No Compris!' There is no evidence that Sassoon replied. The poem draws on Owen's experience of the Allies' 'spring offensive' in April 1917 (Stallworthy, *Owen*, pp. 178–82), and its MSS show that it was never finally revised.

14–15 *buttercups . . . boots*: Harold Owen wrote that his brother had coined the image in 1907, returning through the fields to Shrewsbury after Evensong in Uffington Church: 'Wilfred gently pressed my arm for silence – hesitated a moment and then called quietly back, "Harold's boots are blessed with gold"' (H. Owen, I, 176). It subsequently appeared in 'A Palinode' (lines 17–20; Stallworthy, pp. 77–8 and 218):

But if the sovereign sun I might behold
With condescension coming down benign,
And blessing all the field and air with gold,
Then the contentment of the world was mine.

Cf. also Keats, 'To Autumn' (lines 2–4): 'Close bosom-friend of the maturing sun; / Conspiring with him how to load and bless / With fruit the vines that round the thatch-eaves run'.

18. *They . . . unstirred*: Owen's MS reads: 'All they strange day they breathe like trees unstirred', and one must suppose that he intended to find alternatives for the first four words, which he crossed out.

29–31 *And instantly . . . blood*: Cf. Henri Barbusse, *Under Fire*: 'Abruptly, across all the width of the opposite slope, lurid flames burst forth that strike the air with terrible detonations. In line from left to right fires emerge from the sky and explosions from the ground' (chapter xx, p. 244).

30. *cups*: 'The word *cups* suggests not only shell-holes but also *buttercup[s]* (line 14) and chalices, cups which are used in the Mass to contain the wine which is both a blessing (cf. *blessed with gold*) and sacrificial blood. Having refused the offered blessing of communion with the natural order, the men have become victims sacrificed to an outraged Nature' (Hibberd, p. 135). Dr Ellen Sarot has detected an echo of Genesis 4:10-11: 'The voice of thy brother's blood crieth unto me from the ground. And now art thou cursed from the earth, which hath opened her mouth to receive thy brother's blood from thy hand' (private correspondence).

33. *last high place*: '[A]nother reference to sacrifice – hilltop sacrificial altars were known in ancient times as "high places"' (Hibberd, p. 135).

34. *Breasted . . . up*: Of the variant, and mainly cancelled, forms of this line (see Stallworthy, p. 378), we prefer one first proposed by Welland.

Preface

Drafted probably in May 1918 at Ripon, this was intended as a preface to a collection of poems Owen hoped to publish in 1919 (Stallworthy, *Owen*, pp. 265–6; Stallworthy frontispiece, pp. 535–6. See also Stallworthy, *Survivors' Songs*, p. 78).

3–4 *glory, . . . majesty, dominion, or power*: Cf. Jude 25: 'To the only wise God our Saviour, be glory and majesty, dominion and power, both now and ever.'

8. *elegies*: Owen had considered – and decided against – calling his book 'English Elegies'.

Index of Titles

Ivor Gurney

Isaac Rosenberg

Wilfred Owen

Index of First Lines

Ivor Gurney

Isaac Rosenberg

Wilfred Owen